W9-ASC-690

SKETCHES OF
FUNERAL SERMONS

by

F. E. ERDMAN, AND OTHERS

BAKER BOOK HOUSE
Grand Rapids, Michigan

Reprinted 1965 by
Baker Book House Company

PHOTOLITHOPRINTED BY CUSHING - MALLOY, INC.
ANN ARBOR, MICHIGAN, UNITED STATES OF AMERICA
1969

Preface

This is another volume in the Minister's Handbook Series. It is designed to be an aid to those who are called upon to officiate at funerals.

These sketches, contributed by numerous authors, were compiled and prepared by an anonymous editor. Among those who are known to have furnished sketches for this book are, F. E. Erdman and J. M. Rinker. The continuing demand for helps in the preparing of funeral messages has encouraged the publishers to make this valuable book once more available.

There is an appropriate and satisfying variety in these sketches. There are, for example, sketches for funeral sermons for young and old, for persons of various personalities and characters, and for those who have been brought to death through varying circumstances. There is comfort, warning and admonition.

In addition to the sixty sketches for sermons there are fifty-four carefully selected texts for funeral messages.

The Publishers

CONTENTS

1. Victory over Death by Enlargement
   of the Spiritual Life ....I Cor. 15:55   5
2. The Voice from Heaven ....Rev. 14:13   7
3. Duration of Human Life ....Ps. 90:10   8
4. The Death of a Christian ....Rom. 14:8   10
5. Paul's Review of Life ....II Tim. 4:6-8   12
6. What Is Your Life ....James 4:14   13
7. Death ....I Sam. 20:3   15
8. Death at the Door ....I Sam. 20:3   17
9. Providence ....Rom. 8:28   19
10. Victory through Christ ....I Cor. 15:57   21
11. Walking with Christ in White ....Rev. 3:4   22
12. The Eternal Judgment ....Acts 17:30, 31   24
13. The Death of Saints ....Ps. 116:15   26
14. A Righteous Man's Characterization
    of Death ....Ps. 23:4   27
15. Funeral of a Child ....Matt. 19:14   29
16. Sighing for Immortality ....II Cor. 5:4   30
17. Not Here, but Yonder ....Deut. 12:9   32
18. The Proximity of Death ....I Sam. 20:3   34
19. Life after Death ....Job 14:14   37
20. The Death of a Child ....Gen. 37:30   38
21. The Death of a Child ....II Sam. 12:23   40
22. My Departure ....II Tim. 4:6   41
23. A Song in the Night ....Isa. 12:2   43
24. A Triumphant Death ....I Cor. 15:55-57   45
25. To Die Is Gain ....Phil. 1:21   47
26. Shadows and Sunshine ....John 16:16   48
27. Attractions of Heaven ....John 14:2, 3   50
28. No Night There ....Rev. 22:1   52
29. Preparation for Death ....Isa. 38:1   53
30. The Death of Our Little Ones ....Sol. Songs 6:2   55
31. The Fearfulness of Death ....I Cor. 15:26   56
32. The Shunamite and Her Child ....II Kings 4:26   58
33. Death the Gift of God ....Ps. 127:2   60
34. Raised in Power ....I Cor. 15:43   61
35. The Blessed Encomium ....Matt. 25:21   63
36. My Change ....Job 14:14   65
37. Our Sainted Dead: They Are Living
    Epistles ....II Cor. 3:2   67

38. Christ the Lord of the Dead .... Rom. 14:7   69
39. Funeral Sermon .... Amos 5:8   71
40. Death at the Door .... I Sam. 20:3   73
41. What We Shall Be in Eternity .... Luke 20:36   75
42. Not Death; but Life .... Rom. 14:8   77
43. Satisfied with Life .... Ps. 91:16   79
44. The Saint's Repose .... Ps. 127:2   80
45. Jesus Calling Children through the
    Angel of Death .... Mark 10:14   82
46. The Great Meeting .... Amos 4:12   84
47. Human Life in the Light of Christ's
    Appearing .... Luke 2:29, 30   86
48. The New Jerusalem .... Rev. 21:5   87
49. Shall We Know Each Other in Heaven ... I Thess. 2:19   89
50. Watching for the Master .... Luke 12:37   92
51. A Whole Family in Heaven .... Gen. 7:1   94
52. Man's March to the Grave .... Job 30:23   94
53. The Close of Summer .... Jer. 8:20   96
54. We Are Not Left Comfortless .... John 14:18   97
55. Death Always in Our Path .... I Sam. 20:3   97
56. Posthumous Eloquence .... Heb. 11:4   99
57. The Certainty of Death .... Heb. 9:27   99
58. An Unexpected Requisition .... Luke 12:20   101
59. The Progressive March of Death's
    Conqueror .... Isa. 25:8   102
60. Death Not Destruction, but a Step
    in the Progress of Development .... Matt. 5:17   103
Appropriate Texts for Funeral Sermons   104

SKETCHES OF
FUNERAL SERMONS

Victory over Death by Enlargement
of the Spiritual Life

"O death, where is thy sting? O grave, where is thy victory?"
— I Cor. 15:55

1. We rejoice in the anticipation of the final redemption of the body, and this is well. This body signifies so much to us; it is so useful a servant of our desires, and so good a home wherein to dwell; it is in its best estate, so glorious a temple for the Holy Ghost; its dissolution brings, in appearance at least, so sharp a pang; around the bodily presence of our friends are clustered so many sweet associations, that it is not strange we rejoice at the coming of a time when death shall be vanquished, and that we cry with Paul, in anticipation of that triumph, "O death, where is thy sting? O grave, where is thy victory?" And the thought of that Heavenly land where there shall be no more death comes to us like a cheerful strain of music amid the sad minor tunes of our hours of bereavement.

2. But there is a sense in which we may have the victory before that time. It is by living so much in the Spirit that the death of the body shall not greatly affect us. We may think so constantly of ourselves as Spiritual beings, and so emphasize and expand and enlarge our Spiritual life, as that the life of the flesh shall scarcely appear to be the life of our essential selves.

3. A hint of this sort is given us in the fact that while we feel that all other men must die, we have a strong sense of our own immortality. "All men think all men mortal but themselves." It is because we identify the idea of *self* with that part of us which we cannot see — that is, with our Spirits, which we realize death

5

cannot touch; while we associate the idea of *another* man with his body, which we look upon, and which, from observation of others many times repeated, we know must die. Now, by just so much as we exalt and enlarge the life of the Spirit, do we make that part of us which consciously does not perish, and in which our true selfhood consists, to preponderate; and in the same degree do we cause it to be true that death shall not affect our essential being.

4. It is sometimes a result of lingering illness that it wears away the body until but a shadow is left, while the long discipline of patient suffering purifies and expands the Spiritual man, so that a small part of the complex nature remains for death to take hold upon. In the case of some devoted Christians we have seen pass away, death thus became almost nothing; and in an ever increasing degree is this true of the men who live the life of the Spirit and not the life of the flesh. They who have mortified the body and its sinful tendencies have in advance largely deprived the last enemy of his prey.

5. Has it never perplexed us to see how lightly God appears to regard the death of men? With him it is a very little thing to destroy the life of the body. Why does He, without the least appearance of reluctance, sweep away whole generations by a single stroke of pestilence, overwhelm cities with the outburst of a volcano, or swallow up a populous island with the yawnings of an earthquake? Why is He so unhesitating in thus bringing about what seem to us such awful tragedies? It is because He sees us as Spirits unaffected by death. To Him, death is a mere trifle, not touching our essential being. He views it as we view the dropping of the chrysalis from the butterfly, as the untrammeling of our real life. He perceives it as a mere superficial incident in the development of the Spirit, which is the chief, the continuing entity, the real self. It is because He is Himself a Spirit, wholly unreached by death, and He knows what a Spirit is. God is conscious in Himself of an ever-abiding life which is unaffected by all the changes of nature, the body in which He clothes Himself and manifests His activities in part. He realizes that under all the ebb and flow of this material universe His nature is unchangeably the same. And we are, in like manner, Spirits, created in His image. In the same degree that we know

ourselves true sons of God, and claim our birthright of Spirit-hood, and enter up into his life, will death loose its power over us; and we shall have victory over it, even before our *final triumph* in the resurrection of the just.

The Voice from Heaven

"And I heard a voice from Heaven saying unto me, write: Blessed are the dead which die in the Lord from henceforth."
— Rev. 14:13

I. PATMOS OF THE SOUL.

Heaven's stair-door opened — Celestial scenes meet the ravishing gaze — heavenly choruses fall upon the enraptured ear. A Christian's death the Apocalypse of the soul. Stephen saw Heaven opened, and Jesus *standing* on the portals. Every where else represented as being *seated*—doubtless arises to welcome the first Christian martyr.

II. A VOICE FROM HEAVEN.

Solomon said: important because it is *from heaven*. Perhaps the good who died in the Lord, send this message back to earth. The redeemed give testimony to their heavenly blessedness. The *voice of* loved ones reiterates this heavenly message to their surviving friends.

III. THE MESSAGE WRITTEN.

Write, transmit it to coming generations. It is a message to us today. Not only martyrs and prophets, but all who die in the Lord are blessed. *From hence-forth,* immediately. As the outward man perishes the inward man is renewed. The soul does not sleep with the body but departs at once to be with Christ, when absent from the body, *Yea,* verily—truly. The Spirit echoes back in solemn tones this glorious truth which should animate every heart, thrill every soul and inspire every one to *live in the Lord.*

IV. WHY THEY ARE BLESSED.

1. They rest from their labors. This rest is not idleness,

for this would be loathing to the soul. There is no loafing around the Throne. There shall be a delightful service. "And His servants shall serve him." Rev. 22:3. It will be a service without weariness or fatigue.

2. This will be a rest from: (a) Suffering of bodily pains. (b) Harassing anxiety of mind. (c) Grief and sorrow of heart. (d) Conflicts and trials of life.

V. THE BEARINGS OF LIFE.

1. A very important and practical lesson is taught here, that it is our character at death that determines our blessedness hereafter, and that our future destiny depends upon the life we have lived. Only those who "die in the Lord" shall be happy; but in order to thus die, we must be *in the Lord* before we die.

2. We are also taught the immortal dignity of Christian labor. The influence and work of a Christian never die. What we do for God and humanity will live and work for us after we are gone. The good we do to the least of Christ's disciples will follow us after we are gone. Good men and women never die. Though dead they speak. If we have treasures laid up in Heaven we get only part of our great possession at death, but our "works" and good deeds will follow us in their influence upon others, in moulding their characters and shaping their destinies, even down to the remotest ages of posterity unto the end of time.

Duration of Human Life

"The days of our years are three score years and ten."
— Ps. 90:10

When one dies, how common it is to ask: "How old was he?" How natural, also, to wonder what the number of the days of our years is to be. The duration of human life depends largely on how it is measured.

1. *As measured by the number of years.* The text gives the probable age of those who may be said to have lived

out their days. One-half of all born into the world die in infancy and childhood. It is estimated that of all those who live to be ten years of age, only two-fifths reach the three-score and ten, one in a hundred reaches ninety, and one in a hundred thousand lives a full century. Careful estimates show that the average duration of life of those who reach what is called "old age" cannot be far from three-score and ten. The physical constitution of man indicates, however, that, were it possible to avoid disease and accident and live in absolute conformity to the laws of nature, the average age of the race would be greatly increased. Certain eminent scientists have reached the conclusion that the natural duration of animal life is not less than five times the period of growth. On the basis of this law, a man's natural duration of life should not be less than one hundred years. We are learning more each year how to obey the laws of hygiene; how to avoid and to remove the cause of death; and, more especially, how to protect the delicate, feeble and aged so as to lengthen out their years.

2. *As measured by the circumstances under which we live.* Human life, really, should not be measured by years, but rather by deeds. The advantages of modern civilization lengthen our lives more than the many years of the ancients. A journey that once required a month is now made in a day. Innumerable inventions, now in use save time and help one to accomplish more in the same number of years. The world's progress in knowledge adds to our lives. That which costs years of labor in discovery, we may know in an hour of reading.

3. *As measured by the habits of life.* The industrious gain time, the idle lose it. Time is precious, and a life in which the moments have been utilized is longer than one of the same number of years in which they have been wasted. It is well enough for men to lengthen the number of their years, if they can, but it is better to improve well the moments as they come.

4. *As measured by the purpose of life.* An aimless life, however long, is worth but little. The most successful lives

have been those which have been actuated by some noble purpose. Those who live to make home more sacred, society more refined, mankind more fortunate, the world more enlightened, always live great lives regardless of the number of their years.

5. *As measured by the preparation for the life beyond.* It may be said that to live this life well is to prepare for the life to come. He lives best of all who early chooses the one true foundation and, during life, builds, with approved material, an edifice of character that will endure the storms of time, the fires of the judgment and abide throughout eternity.

The Death of a Christian

"For whether we live, we live unto the Lord; and whether we die, we die unto the Lord; whether we live therefore, or die, we are the Lord's." — Rom. 14:8

The apostle writes against narrow heartedness and human standards of religion, and declares that Christ is the only one object for whom all Christians live, and teaches us in this Scripture

I. THE PRINCIPLE OF SELF-SACRIFICE TO GOD'S SERVICE AND THE WELL-BEING OF OTHERS.

It is a fact, whether recognized or not, that the Christian does not live for himself, "for none of us liveth to himself," but his influence, consciously or unconsciously, goes out over his fellow men.

1. *The great object the Christian has in view, is to live for the Lord.* (a) In public life. (b) In social. (c) In private life. His aim is to glorify the Lord Jesus Christ in his life by all that he does and says, and in all things it is manifest that he "lives unto the Lord." That life alone is successful which is consecrated to God; others may have measurable success, but it does not reach beyond the limits of time, while that of the Christian embraces time and eternity. "For Godliness is profitable unto all things, etc." I Tim. 4:8.

2. *The Christian's life is for others.* If by anything that he can do to alleviate the ills of his fellows, he will do it regardless of what sacrifice it may call forth; his desire is to see men blessed and brought into a saving knowledge of Christ. This Spirit assisted the apostles to journey over land and sea to carry the glad tidings to the hungering masses—this Spirit assisted the first martyrs and reformers—this Spirit assisted Missionaries and others to deny themselves and preach Christ to a lost world—this Spirit assisted many a poor, weak, suffering Christian to patiently do and abide the will of his Master. The Christian being so absorbed in the discharge of his duty and living in such sweet communion with his Master realizes

II. THAT HE IS SECURE AT ALL TIMES AND CAN SAY *"Whether we die we die unto the Lord."* That is, my life belongs unto the Author of life, and as He wills I am satisfied. The sacred writer recognizes:

1. *That there is an overruling providence that governs the affairs of God's children.*

2. *That the life of a Christian is not a life of chance,* but that the everlasting arms of an omnipotent God are underneath him and directs all his ways.

3. *His concern is not so much about his death as it is about his life.* If we live right we shall die right.

III. THE APOSTLE ACKNOWLEDGES THE LORD AS THE RIGHTFUL OWNER OF ALL THAT HE IS AND HAS. "Whether we live therefore, or die, we are the Lord's."

1. *In time,* because— (a) He purchased us, (b) He redeemed us, (c) He sustains us, (d) By His grace we have lived for Him.

2. *In Eternity* because— (a) He promised, "If ye confess me before men I will also confess you before my Father and his Holy Angels." (b) Because of his desire to have His own where he is also. In conclusion,

1. Do you live for the Lord? 2. Do you realize that you are secure and prepared to meet your God? 3. Are you the Lord's?

Paul's Review of Life

"I am now ready to be offered, and the time of my departure is at hand." — II Tim. 4:6-8

Seasons of sorrow come to every heart. We look about us for a sufficient amount of consolation from earthly friends, but such sympathy as comes from such a source does not satisfy. We listen to expressions of comfort that come from our most intimate friends, but how empty and unsatisfactory these words are. We look above us and see a future full of brightness, and hear a voice that is full of sweetness. It is the voice of inspiration—it comes to us as a revelation, and today we recognize in this text of Scripture the saintly voice of the greatest men the church of God has ever known. He occupies one of the most exalted positions, for viewing life aright, that can possibly be found. Prospectively death is not distant, and he therefore desires to get a three-fold view of life.

I. *The life which is past*—Just the kind of life we are living today. (1) He regards it as a *fight*. The whole human race thus regard life: but the Christian looks upon it as *a good fight*. A fight always implies opposition, here from the *world*, the *flesh* and *satan*. We meet it in early life: it continues even to the time of our "departure."

But the Apostle calls this a good fight—why? Because it is for God and right—no other can be good. It is also "a fight of faith." "Our weapons are not carnal, but mighty through God, to the pulling down of the strong holds" of sin and satan. Our success does not depend upon our strength or skill, but on something infinitely better—our "faith in God." Paul said at the close of life, "I have kept the faith," may we be able to say as much when the hour of death draws near.

II. *The life which now is*—the present. He says "I am now ready to be offered." I have the blessed assurance that (1) My work on earth is done (2) My time to depart has come (3) I am ready to go. O what a complete experience is this. "Happy if with our latest breath" we too may give expression to language so full of thrill and joy. With some of us the sun of life is setting—the day will soon be gone—the night of death is near: but

> "The stream is calmest when it nears the tide,
> And flowers are sweetest at the eventide;
> And birds most musical at close of day,
> And saints divinest when they pass away."

III. The life which is to come—the future. He anticipates it, and says, "Henceforth there is laid up for me a crown of righteousness." We, each of us, *desire* such a crown. But do we fully *expect* it? Bishop Morris says "It takes both desire and expectation to produce Christian hope," which hope is an anchor, both sure and steadfast. Notice particularly the facts that comforted the author of our text in the face of death, and we shall fiind that they are the same facts that can comfort us. He says,

1. I have a crown *laid up* in heaven—"where moth and rust doth not corrupt."

2. He believes it is *kept for him,* because, "God is able to keep that which we commit to Him."

3. He expects it to be given to him in that day, by the Judge himself. A personal gift, of priceless worth. Let us each remember how he came in possession of this crown, and in like manner secure such treasure for ourselves.

What Is Your Life?

"Whereas ye know not what shall be on the morrow. For what is your life? It is even a vapour, that appeareth for a little time, and then vanisheth away." — James 4:14

The present life is lived under the shadows of constant change. The present constitution of society from its extreme selfishness makes it impossible to enjoy much, while oppression, and adversity dominate. This has much to do with the failures on every hand to carry out good resolutions, generous impulses, noble aspirations and to perfect Christian manliness. The vast majority sink under the uneven pressure, and abandon even the thought of a possible Christ-like life. "The world lieth in darkness." The lust of the flesh, the lust of the eyes and the pride of life," "shut up the bowels of compassion" "one against the other," and there is but little love. Gen. 47:9. In the midst of all this, men and women assume to treat life as though they had supreme control of it, and James' question is timely to show that a time cometh when "the morrow." need not be expected. Since God controls and has all to say about the beginning and end of all life, his question also indicates:

I. WHAT THE TRUE OBJECT OF LIFE IS.

In spite of existing troubles, there is an object of living beyond that which is purely secular and selfish. Nor is it a *chance* object. It is an end of living in perfect harmony with man's creation. It points toward a possible reunion of man with God in a differently constructed state of society. One that is pure, disinterested, incorruptible and interminable. Its only attainment is by means of a Supreme recognition of, and service to God through Christ. This is the God-directed end of every well organized life, and man does his duty only in the ratio that he makes this his solemn purpose. Such a life cannot be wrecked. II Peter 1-11.

II. SUCH A LIFE IS DIFFICULT TO LIVE.

The conflicting state of affairs all about us make it so. Yet, in the midst of this darkness the chief end of all living shines with all the more splendor. The painter fills the background of his picture with heavy colors to give prominence to it, and so with the Christian life in the midst of the world's darkness, its trials and oppression. We are called upon to do the same in hope of "recompense of reward." Heb. 5:8, 9; 12:2; 11:26. Those who "endure" come to their end, like a sunset in solemn majesty. Psa. 116:15. Rev. 14:13. Fighting a good fight and keeping the faith, is the road to all of this.

III. WHAT SHOULD BE OUR CHIEF AMBITION.

Not what shall we eat, drink, and wear. But seeking the Kingdom of God in right living. "Seek ye first the Kingdom etc." God assumes responsibilities; these He discharges in his own best way. He has given us a model of success after which to pattern, *i.e.,* His Son. Paul followed him and *won.* II Tim. 14:6-8. See his chief ambition. Phil. 3:8-15. Such a life ends in giving us a knowledge of ourselves we could not have in any other way, and in the end life forevermore.

Reflections: 1. Brother, sister, "what is your life?" Is it worldly, Christless, promiseless, hopeless? Or is it God-like, faithful, full of the promise of coming victory? 2. My alien friend will you not abandon the world with its deception, its tinselry and sorrows? Will you not believe in Christ; repent of your sins; confess his name; be baptized upon His authority, and labor to reproduce His life in your own, for the hope of eternal life? See Mark 16:15, 16; Acts 2:38; Rom. 10:9; Col. 3:1, 2. Thus you will make your life what it ought to be, and rejoice in prospect of a life to come.

Death

"There is but a step between me and death" — I Sam. 20:3

Jealousy, anger and an unfriendly demeanor, harbored in the heart and mind of King Saul, and the thrusting forth upon several occasions the fury of his heart against David, his son-in-law, exposed the life of the latter to jeopardy and uncertainty. Hence the sorrowful words of the text by David to his friend and brother-in-law Jonathan. Among all the created things which man holds in his possession, there is nothing so uncertain to him as his life, and nothing so absolutely positive as his death. The deist may believe in God and deny his revealed religion. And the infidel may continue in his unbelief concerning a hereafter. But none of these dare venture the theory and preach to mankind that man need not die.

I. THE CAUSE OF DEATH.

1. By referring to the word of God for our guide we need not be ignorant concerning the cause of death; six thousand years ago when man lived in his primeval state of happiness in Eden when death was yet wholly unknown to him, God

visited him and placed upon him His divine fiat. Gen. 2:16, 17. And the Lord God commanded the man, saying, "of every tree of the garden thou mayest freely eat, . . . thou shalt surely die." We read in Gen. 3:6, that this injunction was grossly violated. Satan became man's tempter. But whereas God can not lie, He was therefore necessitated to bring to pass upon the entire human family the fulfillment of His command.

2. The violation of God's injunction as stated is the cause of every death. Rom. 5:12.

3. This cause of death can never be removed from the race of mankind; though Christ through His vicarious suf-ferings, and sacrificial death, restored again the soul of man into the favor of God, yet He could not, or did not, exoner-ate man from his natural death. Gen. 6:17.

II. THE NEARNESS TO DEATH.

1. The text describes it as but a "step" between life and death. Job 8:9; Job 14:1, 2; Ps. 90; James 4:14. The strong may boast of his strength, the cambist of his wealth, and the philosopher of his wisdom; but the certainty of life is among the unknown. "Truly," etc.

2. Death is near to all; to the infant, to the youth, to the middle aged, and the aged. 86,400 die every twenty-four hours. Therefore, the solemn interrogatory, who will be called upon by the *grave monster, death, to* swell tomorrow's number?

3. Death may be very near to us when we are in our most vigorous and most healthful days, and when in our own presumption we put it into the far off future.—Nadab, Alihu, Haman, Beltshazzar, and others.

III. THE PREPARATION FOR DEATH.

1. To this great end, viz: the preparation for death, there is but one thing necessary. That we forsake sin, and turn to the Lord, and become wholly His. John 3:3. Titus 3:5.

2. Knowing therefore this brevity and frailty of life, it behooves all mankind to make due preparation for death. Rom. 6:12.

3. When should such preparation be sought? Now, Paul says Heb. 4:7. "Today," etc.

4. The young, the middle-aged, and the aged should seek this preparation; just as we are liable to die in these different stages of life, so should we seek the preparation for death in these stages.

5. Only a true preparation can produce a tranquil death. Therefore the Prophet Amos has well said, Amos 4:12. "Prepare to meet thy God."

Application. 1. You must die. 2. You must appear before God. 3. You will be rewarded according to your deeds while in the body. 4. What are your prospects?

Death at the Door

"There is but a step between me and death." — I Sam. 20:3

If there is but a step between me and death, then what will become of me when I die? "Man dieth and wasteth away, man giveth up the ghost," and where is he? It is a question of the greatest importance: where is he? This must be a serious consideration to you and to me.

There is this consequence which is involved in it. If there is but a step between me and death, then how important it is to be prepared for death! It is possible to be prepared to die. A person may be so prepared to die, that death will never come to him strangely or unacceptably.

There is another consequence resulting from this statement: If there is but a step between us and death, then how precious is life! What great and tender care should be taken of it! A sinner does not live half his days; he exists but he does not live; he has none of the pure enjoyment of life.

Read the sixty-third Psalm, and you will see what it is to live in association with God, in communion with him who made us, and in the delights of His most gracious presence. A life compared to the richest luxuries and dainties, of which the palate is capable of tasting: "My soul shall be satisfied as with marrow and fatness; and my soul shall praise Thee with joyful lips: when I remember Thee upon my bed, and meditate on Thee in the night watches." What an invaluable and incomparable thing, then, is time in relation to life! How much rests on its right improvement and use! My friends, it is a thing which we may lose in an hour, in a moment. How highly then, should it be prized at all times. And the lesson comes, under the circumstances connected with this sermon, with a double emphasis to every one present. Life, then, is not to be squandered, but to be improved; not to be degraded by sin, but to be exalted by righteousness. Use it for God and "whatsoever thy hand findeth to do, do it with thy might for there is no work, nor device, nor knowledge, nor wisdom in the grave, whither thou goest."

If there is but a step between us and death, then let us care for the salvation and happiness of those whom we leave behind. If life is so uncertain, everything should be done for others within our power; we should endeavor to render them happy after we die. "Am I my brother's keeper?" someone asks. That is the language of Cain, and we should not like to be placed in the situation and circumstances of Cain. No man who has a deep interest in the welfare of his fellowman, can ever utter that language. Seeing that circumstances may soon bring you to the mouth of the grave, I ask you solemnly today, are you employing those efforts for God which you might do? Are you teaching in a Sunday school, or distributing tracts? Are you useful in your family? Are you employing those talents which God has given you in some humble way, in order to circulate the Gospel of salvation? Oh! carry home these questions with you today; and while you think seriously of them, say, "While there is but a step between me and death, as long as that step exists, it shall find me engaged in the service of my Lord and Master."

Finally, if there is but a step between us and death, let those continually exposed to danger be alive to the importance of the present moment. Let the solemn resolve of your hearts, on going from this house of sorrow be, "Seeing that there is but a step between me and death," "As for me and my house we will serve the Lord."

Providence

"All things work together for good to them that love God. . . ."
— Rom. 8:28

It is man's natural disposition to murmur at the wise dispensations of providence. God's will seldom seems to be man's will, and the Spirit of Job's wife, ubiquitous, and immortal, comes down upon the wings of 3000 years, and prompts the sorrow stricken to curse his God and die. The text is wonderfully expressive, and suggestive.

I. ALL THINGS.

There is no more comprehensive phrase than this, "all things." It includes everything of which we can have the slightest possible conception; everything in earth, and in Heaven, and Hell; things natural and Spiritual, nominal and real, all are included in the term "all things."

II. ALL THINGS WORK.

There is constant activity in nature, there is nothing that is passive. The same thing is true in grace. The first time God is introduced to the world, He is introduced as a *working* being. "In the beginning God created," etc. The Holy Ghost is constantly at *work*, correcting, converting and regenerating the sinner, confessing, guiding and sanctifying the saint. Jesus Christ was a *working* being. "He went about continually doing good." And so it is true, both in nature and grace, that "all things work."

III. ALL THINGS WORK TOGETHER.

There is not only constant activity in nature, but there is constant *harmony* there. One law does not counteract the influence of another law, but all work in unison. The same thing is true in grace; what God has done the Son has perpetuated, what the Son has perpetuated the Holy Ghost has completed; and thus in nature and grace, all things work, and work together in harmony.

IV. ALL THINGS WORK TOGETHER FOR GOOD.

1. *Temptations* are for good: "Blessed is he that endureth temptation," etc.

2. *Persecutions* are for good: "Blessed are they that are persecuted," etc.

3. *Poverty* is for good: There are special promises made to the poor. "Behold the lilies of the field," etc.

4. *Afflictions* are for good: "These light afflictions which are bent for a moment," etc.

5. *Death* is for good: "Blessed are the dead who die in the Lord," etc.

V. THIS PROMISE MADE TO THOSE WHO LOVE GOD.

1. *What is it to love God. 2. What is "God's purpose?" 3. What are the evidences of this love?*

VI. THIS PROMISE IS IMPOSSIBLE FOR THE SINNER TO BELIEVE.

1. Because they judge God's providences from *a carnal* standpoint. "God's thoughts are not as our thoughts, nor His ways as our ways."

2. They judge God's providences *selfishly*. They think that because they are not *pleasant*, that therefore they are not profitable.

3. They judge God's providences *prematurely*. We have no right to condemn a song, until we hear it sung. No right to condemn a picture, until the last finishing touches are put upon it. Wait! Patience is a godly virtue. Wait! It is a divine command. "Wait on the Lord, be of good courage, and He will strengthen thine heart, wait I say, on the Lord."

Victory through Christ

"Thanks be to God, which giveth us the victory through our Lord Jesus Christ." — I Cor. 15:57

The cloud which gathers over the close of the Christian's day has a silver lining. When we take our stand by the silent form, or at the open grave, it is all dark. The broken link, the vacant chair, the silent voice have about them the chill of November. But if with the eye of faith we sweep the upward way, along which there are trailings of that glory which is now complete; and stand with the conqueror beside the Savior, we see nothing but sunshine. We are in the balminess of the Springtime of the soul. It is because of this faith, that Paul writes with such confidence. He sees

I. *Victory.* It is lamentable how even Christians speak of death. To the Savior the departed one has fallen asleep. To Paul the same thought encourages him to endure the sufferings of this present life. We speak of the loss, the vacancy, the sorrow. Paul speaks of victory. It would seem according to our accustomed expressions, that the departed have been overcome. With the eye of faith we ought to speak of victory for the dying Christian, with the same confidence that we speak of the victorious death of Christ. Let us get out of the chill of death and the grave, into the warmth and glow of the heavenly life, upon which our beloved has entered.

II. *His victory is through Jesus Christ.*

The popular philosophy of the day, conceives man as attaining his full stature of manhood, thought, natural forces. He has an environment that furnishes all that is needed for the development of his body, soul and spirit. The same theory colors much of our religious thought. It lacks in loyalty to Christ. United with Christ, buried with Christ and risen with Christ were the watchwords of him who could say thanks be to God, which giveth us the victory through our Lord Jesus Christ.

III *Because of this victory men should be*

1. *Steadfast.* Not cast about by every wind of doctrine—

not timid and fearful and unbelieving, but with steady step walk in the way of the commandments of the Lord.

2. *Unmovable*, with the assurance of such a victory, through Christ, he stands upon a solid rock. Death cannot separate him from the love of God.

3. *Always abounding in the work of the Lord.* As little as the flowers can resist the sunshine in spring time, can the Christian, filled with this blessed hope, fail to respond to the work which the Lord commits to his hands.

Walking with Christ in White

"Thou hast a few names even in Sardis which have not defiled their garments...." — Rev. 3:4

I. THE PERSON SPEAKING.

Christ himself—the true and faithful witness; who knows the condition, and *"works"* of every man.

II. THE PERSON SPOKEN OF.

They are those who "have not defiled their garments"—who have not sullied the purity of their Christian life or character, which is here regarded as a white robe of right-eousness—They are those—

1. *Whose garments were once stained with sin*—"All have sinned."

2. *Whose sins were forgiven, whose garment stains were all washed away "in the blood of the Lamb," by Repentance and Faith*—The only effectual remedy for sin, for all men.

3. *Who kept their garments clean in the midst of much uncleanness, and many temptations.* They were "not defiled." This proves what many deny, the possibility of being saved from all sin, and leading a holy life in this present world.

III. WHAT IS SAID OF THEM—"They shall walk with me in white."

1. *These words relate to their Heavenly state.*

2. *Their state in the other world corresponds with the character they maintained on the earth*—So will our state.

These words teach further—

1. *That Heaven is a place*—"*they shall walk.*"

2. *That it is a state or condition "of life—liberty."* (a). *Of perfect purity.* "Walk in white." (b). *Of unmingled and uninterrupted joy*—"With me." As in the cool of the morning we walk for health and pleasure. So also in the pleasant walks of the Heavenly Paradise. (c). *Of activity and progression*— "Walk" not of idleness, but constant employment. Progression "from glory to glory." (d). *Of exquisite beauty and grandeur* —"White flowing garments of the redeemed." What must the place itself be?

THE REASON ASSIGNED. "For they are worthy."

1. Not that they have any claim to, or worthiness for Heaven, on the ground of their own merit, or, that it will be in virtue of their own works.

2. But they have the character to which God has promised eternal life, and according to the arrangement of grace it is but fit and proper that they should be received there. It is not a legal, but a gospel worthiness, not merit, but meetness. A worthiness put on them by Christ himself here. Worthiness *in Christ,* clothed in His Righteousness, filled with His Spirit, characterized and prompted by His Love to self-denial and holiness of heart and life.

3. Having made Christ their choice, and having faithfully served Him, and suffered with and for Him in the world, they now rest and rejoice with Him in Heaven. They who walk with Christ in the clean garments of real practical holiness here, and keep themselves unspotted from the world, shall walk with Him also in white robes of honor and glory in the world to come. What is the character of our life?

The Eternal Judgment

"The times of this ignorance God winked at, but now commanded all men everywhere to repent...." — Acts 17:30, 31

Concerning the "eternal judgment" the popular presumption is certainly at fault. Two theories are prevalent—if they may be called such. The first is, that on a certain day of twenty-four hours, or of dispensational length, God will *personally* enter into judgment with every person ever having lived. The second is that this judgment is now in progress with each individual, ending at his death. Both are baseless notions. They make no exception for the heathen, barbarian, any type of human brute, or for infants or idiots. They are right in but one thing which is that there will be a judgment.

I. *Some have lived and died for whom the judgment will have no terrors.* It may be that certain ones could not in harmony with justice be brought into judgment for salvation or condemnation. Psalm 49:6-20; Mal. 4:3.

11. *Human responsibility arises out of human capacity to discern good and evil.* Not only so, but to *act* on it also. If this is not true, "what is truth?" John 16:24; also, John 15:22.

III. *The doctrine of eternal judgment is fundamental.* It is one of the "first principals" of the oracles. Heb. 6:2. It should, therefore, be understood. In order to do this it must be viewed in the light of the inter-relations between God and man. Here we must keep to the record, else all is speculation.

IV. *There were many steps in the plan of redemption.* This points to different degrees of light possessed and consequent varied relations, all having an essential bearing on the coming judgment. This must not be lost to sight. There was a time when God "winked" at sin. Acts 17:30. This was because of lack of light. People then followed and ended in *their* own ways. Acts 14:16. Their death was their judgment. Rom. 1:32. The circumstances and capacities of people have all to do with their relations to the "judgment to come." Rom. 4:15. "If ye were blind, (ignorant), ye should have no sin." John 9:41. "Man that is in honor and *understandeth* not, is like the beasts that *perish*." "This is the *ground* of condemnation (judgment), that light is come. . . ." John 3:19.

V. *The absence of light changes the ground of amenability.* Abraham in the midst of idolatry, has not the responsibilities of Abraham in covenant. The requirement is greater under the latter circumstances. "To whom men gave much, they require more." Some will receive "few stripes," others "many stripes." Contrast the opportunities, privileges, and relations of people from Adam to the Cross.

VI. *From the days of calvary, the relations of people to the judgment have changed.* The full light now shines. Christ is the light that lightens every man. Human sinfulness and accountability asserted now as never before. Christ is the pivot and means of the coming judgment. John 5:22. The word of God is the rule. John 12:48.

VII. *Who, therefore, should fear the judgment?* An important but easily answered question. In taking out of the world a "people for his name," the invitation has gone to the ends of the earth. "Many are called, but (in judgment), few are chosen." The net encloses "good" and "bad." There are faithful and unfaithful servants. Different degrees of fruit born. Some "sow sparingly," others "bountifully;" some bring forth thirty, some sixty, others a hundred fold. No *man* can assess the degrees. To attempt it is *ruin.* This is the purpose of the judgment. As Paul says, it "begins at the house of God." The follower of Christ, then, is the one who has cause to fear on account of his relations to God through Christ, "lest a promise being left," etc.

Reflections: Comforting to think that a time cometh when all injustice will be exposed. True worth and unappreciated merit recognized. All shames uncovered. Hence, God now "commands all men everywhere to repent, because" of this appointed day and tribunal. Brother, sister, impenitent sinner, every one must then give an account of himself to God, and receive for the things done, *in the body,* whether good or bad.

The Death of Saints

"Precious in the sight of the Lord is the death of his Saints."
— Ps. 116:15

"The death of Saints is an object of value." God regards it of importance; it is connected with His great plans, and there are great purposes to be accomplished by it. The death of a good man is in itself of so much importance, and so connected with the Glory of God and the accomplishment of His purposes, that he will not cause it to take place except under circumstances, at times and in a manner which will best secure those ends. God does not decide on this hastily, or without the best reasons. The act of removing a good man from the world, is an act of deep deliberation on the part of God; He regards it with special interest; it is the removal of another of the redeemed to Glory.

It is a new triumph of the work of redemption, showing the power and the value of that work. It often furnishes a more direct proof of the reality of religion, than any abstract argument could do. See how the cause of religion has been promoted by the patient deaths of Latermer, Ridley, Huss and others.

What an argument for the truth of religion; what an illustration of its sustaining power; what a source of comfort to us who are soon to die—to reflect that religion does not leave the believer when he most needs its support and consolation. That it can sustain us in our severest trial, that it can illuminate what seems to us of all places most dark, the valley of the shadow of death.

But the death of saints is precious in the sight of the Lord, because they are His own children, they have been bought with a price, not with corruptible things, with silver and gold, but with the precious blood of Christ.

We have met here today to express to each other our common affliction for our friend who was taken from us; but we may yet hope to see him again where sorrow and parting are no more.

A Righteous Man's Characterization of Death

"Yea though I walk through the valley of the shadow of death. . . ." — Ps. 23:4

David was a man after God's own heart, and such men's dying differs decidedly from those who know not God. David had repented of his sins, and the Lord had accepted him, and hence he speaks with so much assurance about his dying.

I. DAVID SPEAKS OF DEATH AS A "SHADOW."

It is somewhat remarkable that such a characterization of death could have been made so long before the advent of Him who "abolished death and brought life and immortality to light." Looking at death today, through the medium of New Testament revelation, in contrast with what it once was before the "Prince of Life" removed its sting and dread, we are fully assured that death is now but a shadow of what it was then. But David speaks in no comparative sense whatever—he denominates death itself *"a shadow."* This characterization at once so advanced and unique, in the face of the unspeakable superstition then prevalent, was only possible by one who lived near to God. A SHADOW! Others speak of the "dust of death," the "fear of death," the "gates of death," the "chambers of death," and the "dominion of death;" but David sees in it *only a shadow.* A shadow is possible only where there is light to produce it, and so David because the Lord was his light, regarded death no more than a shadow. "The Lord is my light and my salvation—of whom shall I be afraid?" *Afraid!* not indeed of death! for a shadow, when it is fully known to be such, has in it, nothing to be afraid of. A shadow is empty and powerless.

II. DAVID REPRESENTS DEATH AS A VALLEY.

A *valley*—not a bleak and barren desert, not a storm crowned mountain, not a foaming, tempest-lashed sea. It is a quiet, serene, solemn valley. It is the peaceable valley at the foot of the "Delectable Mountains" of a holy life. He who walks on the heights of Beulah in a daily, steady, progressive walk with God, shall also walk in all holy composure with Jehovah in the illuminated valley of the shadow of death. Many people read into this passage a qualifying word for which David is not responsible, since he did not put it there. It is the word "dark"—The *"dark* valley." But the valley David speaks of is one that shall be to the righteous full of the richest, ripest, golden harvest of promise, and so not a dark valley.

III. DAVID CHARACTERIZES DEATH AS A TRANSIENT "WALK."

David expected only to "walk *through"* this shadow and valley of death. Soul-sleeping was not a part of David's creed, for he lived while he walked and walked while he lived in this fearless shadow and quiet valley. Though our bodies go down into the cold shadowy grave, our spirits shall rise out of the shadows which have fallen upon the body; nay, even the body itself shall soon come up again to be "fashioned like unto Christ's own glorious body."

IV. DAVID CHARACTERIZES DEATH AS AN EXALTED COMMUNION.

What an unspeakable wealth of meaning is contained in these words: "Thou art with me, thy rod and thy staff they comfort me." To have God with us in duty, in adversity, etc., this is the sum and glory of all possessions." But oh, to have the "Great Shepherd" walk with us in "the valley of the shadow of death!" The Great Shepherd is the best companion to have in the shadowy valley. He knows all about its windings, shadows, and dangers. For three days and three nights he walked up and down in it himself, and ever since he has been the light and guide of those who in his name have journeyed that way. His presence, in life as in death, has inspired countless millions with comfort and cheer. Trust Him in life and His "rod and staff" will comfort you in death.

Funeral of a Child

"But Jesus said, suffer little children, and forbid them not, to come unto me; for such is the Kingdom of Heaven."
— Matt. 19:14

Jesus the God-man is represented to us in the Scriptures as bearing a three-fold relation, to His people, of Prophet, Priest and King. The idea of His priest-hood is involved in the text.

I. THE PRIEST-HOOD OF CHRIST.

1. Implies His sacrificial offering upon the cross for sin —once for all.

2. His intercession for all as Mediator before the Father's Throne. "Five bleeding wounds he bears," etc.

3. As a faithful High Priest that can be touched with the feelings of our infirmities, enters into the feelings and sympathies of human nature. He was *human*—very man. The experience of every troubled and sorrow-stricken heart touches His sympathetic nature. He wept at the grave of Lazarus. He stands by the grave of your loved ones to comfort and sustain you as He did the sisters of Lazarus.

II. WHY JESUS TOOK A SPECIAL INTEREST IN CHILDREN.

1. Because He honored and sanctified infancy and child-hood. He was the babe of Bethlehem.

2. Because He gave the children their existence. He takes an interest in the welfare of those who form a great part of his noblest work.

3. Because He has redeemed them. Children need the atoning merits of His precious blood as well as adults. And in some unexplainable way Jesus washes their hearts from the gilt of original depravity, and fits their souls for the Mansions of Eternal bliss in Heaven.

4. Because of the infinite value of an immortal Spirit. We sometimes say, "only a child," yet the infant mind, though of meagre intelligence, has capacities that are capable of infinite development.

5. *For of such is the Kingdom of Heaven.* Truly none but children get Heaven; for Jesus tells us we must all become as little children or we can not enter that blessed place.

III. THE DUTY OF PARENTS.

1. Bring your children to Jesus while young in life. Like Hannah, consecrate them to the Lord from infancy. God speaks to every mother, as Pharaoh's daughter spoke to the mother of Moses: Ex. 2:9. Christian nurture and discipline insure a rich reward in this life and the life to come.

2. The children belong to Heaven; then rejoice, though death has snatched them from your fond embrace, that they have only gone home before you. The gardener has only plucked a flower from earth to bloom in the Paradise of Heaven.

Sighing for Immortality

"For we that are in this tabernacle do groan, being burdened...." — II Cor. 5:4

Every individual born into this world, walks in a path peculiarly his own. No one can forecast it for him—none can trace in advance the number of its windings, its abrupt turns, its tedious mountain passes, or its deep, heavily-shaded, dread-awakening valley wanderings. The millions that have passed before have left no such impress upon the molding influences of time, as to enable us even to approximate in any prediction what the individual will be in this or that period or adventure. One life of a few fleeting years—what a volume it composes! And, in many respects, how different every life seems to be from every other that has ever been lived before!

But all the infinity of the different paths in which individuality is moving, converge at last—all, whether honored or in dishonor, whether cultured or uncultured, literate or illiterate, rich or poor—come down to

THE COMMON GOAL

As Raleigh has well said: "Oh, eloquent, just and mighty

death! Those whom none could advise, thou hast persuaded; what none hath dared, thou hast done; and whom all the world flattered, thou only hast cast out and despised. Thou hast drawn together all the far-stretched greatness, all the pride, cruelty and ambition of man and covered it over with those two narrow words—'Here lies!'" Shirley has expressed the same thought in these striking lines:

"The glories of our blood and state,
    Are shadows, not substantial things;
There is no armor against fate,
    Death lays his icy hands on Kings;
        Scepter and Crown,
        Must tumble down,
And in the dust, be equal made,
With the poor, crooked Scythe and Spade."

In the context of our subject, our frail, mortal body is compared to a tabernacle—a temporary shelter and protection used by travelers in their journey. It is portable, now here, then removed and pitched elsewhere. It is not a permanent residence, not a home; but it fittingly illustrates the instability of our mortal state. Weighed down with infirmities, diseases, afflictions, sufferings and disappointments; St. Paul could not any more strikingly express it than in the words of our text: "In this *tabernacle* indeed we groan, being burdened." Lest he might be misunderstood, however, he explains: "Not that he would be unclothed"—not that we are desirous of death for *death's sake,* as the atheist might desire it; but for that which is *beyond the grave*—"Not that we would be unclothed, *but clothed upon that mortality might be swallowed up of life."* The Christian does not seek more mortality, but

HE SIGHS FOR MORE LIFE,

a thought thrillingly expressed by Pope in these lines:

"Vital spark of Heavenly flame,
Quit, O quit this mortal frame,
Trembling, hoping, lingering, flying,
O the pain, the bliss of dying!
Cease fond nature, cease the strife,
And let me languish into life!"

Those who are without hope when the infirmities and burdens of life become intolerable, must seek death for death's sake; but the Christian looks upon death as *the door into life.* This thought is the secret of "the bliss of dying."

"IN THIS WE GROAN."

The mortal limitation becomes too circumscribed for the fulness of the expanding soul—She feels oppressed, imprisoned, and sighs for larger liberties. As with the caged eagle, the motions of the soaring faculty smite against the bars, and vision falters not before a brilliancy whose glory fills immensity. The powers of an immortal mind reach out for more field, more reality, more glory, more divinity. When this is fully realized, it will be,

THE DEATH OF DEATH.

Mortality will be swallowed up of life forever.

Not Here, but Yonder!

"For ye are not as yet come to the rest ... which the Lord your God giveth you." — Deut. 12:9

How prone we are to expect rest where no rest is, and to seek an inheritance among things doomed to sudden decay! But hearken, O Christian Pilgrims—travelers in the world's wilderness, with a Heavenly Canaan beyond the Jordan of death, to these words, full of the profoundest warning and divinest love. *"Ye are not as yet come to the rest and to the inheritance which the Lord your God giveth you!"* The soul's rest and inheritance, not here, but yonder! What evidence have we for the statement being true?

I. No mortal man has ever yet had real peace in this world; or come into an inheritance which fully satisfied him. Here, human desires are baulked on every side; limited and circumscribed by the vanity and nothingnesses of this world. The man who wears a sovereign's crown is not satisfied; neither is the beggar that sits in the dust—nor the millionaire, nor philosopher, nor the gayest member of the fashionable multitude, nor the idiot! As one or other of these, no man can find rest to his weary Spirit, nor an inheritance appeasing his insatiable cravings! A man may uncomplainingly put up with his lot in this world, whether it be poverty or riches, toil or leisure, but in it he has not perfect happiness. The horse is satisfied here; so is the dog; the bird that builds its nest under our eaves; the fish that gambles in the brook; and the lion in his native jungle—all these have come to their rest and inheritance. But there is a being on this earth who can not be appeased. It is man. Air will not satisfy him—nor water, nor fire, nor gold, scholarship, pleasure, power, fame! O there are desires in my soul that leap the boundaries of all terrestial things, rolling along a boundless Eternity. Not *here* can be my rest and inheritance, but *yonder!* What is not Eternal must ever remain unequal to me!

II. The second reason for the true things of the soul not being *here*, but *yonder,* is to be found in the fact that this earth is going to be destroyed. Isa. 51:6; Matt. 24:35; II Peter 3:10; Rev. 21:1, 2. The truth here taught lies in the nature of things. Man destroys the things which he has made when they have served his purpose. The Almighty created this globe for a purpose. When that purpose has been accomplished, the fires will blaze, the rocks will smoke and the present aspect of things will vanish—*a new earth will not be the old earth!* This being the case, our lasting possessions can not be here, they must be *yonder!*

III. A third reason comes from the pen of the great Preacher— (Eccl. 12:5) *"Because man goeth to his long home, and the mourners go about the streets."* Brooklyn is a city of nearly one million. But all about us are crowded cities of the dead! Greenwood, Evergreen, Calvary, Woodlawn, Cypress Hill, etc. O how rapidly these resting places of the departed are being populated! How numerous are the sorrowing processions that roll along these streets! How often the newly upturned earth of the "narrow house" is surrounded by mourning friends and bleeding hearts! How familiar are the words—"earth to earth," "ashes to ashes," "dust to dust" —reminding us that not *here,* but *yonder,* must be our rest

and inheritance. The Scriptures abound with passages showing the truth before us: *that the true estate of the soul cannot
be in this life.* Job 14:1, 2; Ps. 103:15, 16; Ps. 39:4-6.

IV. The rest not being here, it must be *yonder.* We are
not left to speculate about the *"yonder."* John 14:1, 2; Heb.
4:9; II Cor. 5:1-6; I Peter 1:3-5; Rev. 14:13. The Gospel
Trumpet gives no uncertain sound about the place of the
soul's true home.

V. God is always seeking to have us live, not for the
"here," but for the "yonder." While we may be gay with the
world's glory; charmed with the world's light and flowers
and gold and apparently satisfied with our place and portion
in this life, our Heavenly Father would, by afflictions, tears
and disappointments, lead us to contemplate and admire and
long for the rest and inheritance to which we have not yet
come.

All through the wilderness journey Moses held up to Israel
the exceeding greatness of the Promised Land. So does the
Bible place Heaven before all its readers. We **have learned but**
little of its wonderful teachings, if our hearts have not glowed
with the grandeur of the prospect that is before us. Rest is
there! O what a thought to the weary, the worn, the broken-
hearted! The "inheritance incorruptible and undefiled and
that fadeth not away" is there "reserved in Heaven for you
who are kept by the power of God through Faith unto
Salvation!"

The Proximity of Death

"But truly as the Lord liveth and as thy soul liveth, there is
but a step between me and death." — I Sam. 20:3

Introduction: Every life embraces experiences which serve
to emphasize certain important facts. David, pursued by the
jealous, envious, malignant Saul who hoped to perpetuate
his kingdom by the destruction of his rival, accepted this
circumstance as a warning of the uncertainty of life and com-

municated his conviction in the most positive manner, to his friend Jonathan. Repeated experiences have brought similar warnings to us, making the declaration in the text appropriate to our case.

We consider:

I. A POSITIVE DECLARATION OF A POSITIVE FACT. It would be difficult to add to the emphasis of David's utterance. "Truly as the Lord liveth, and thy soul liveth," lays unusual stress upon the fact stated. Many of the accepted truths relative to life and death are put in equivocal forms of expression. They have not been entirely freed from doubt. The possibility of their controversion is recognized. The significant truth of the text, the proximity of death, is not of this class. It required and was furnished the most direct and positive form of utterance.

David knew that his life lay along the borderline of the death-land.

God's Word sets for this truth in beautiful but forceful imagery. "They are as a sleep. In the morning they are like grass which groweth up. In the morning it flourisheth and groweth up; in the evening it is cut down and withereth." The tender grass blade, the budding, blossoming flower, the shifting wind, the subtle and ever fleeing shadow, are commissioned to preach to us the brevity and uncertainty of life, the certainty of death.

The intricate and delicate character of our physical organism tells us the same fact. Heart-beats are messages; the pulsation of the blood as it bounds along its appointed way, tells us of death; the quiet imperceptible breath speaks of the nearness of life's end.

The destructive agencies present and active everywhere repeat the same message. The means we employ for our comfort, may quickly and easily become our destroyers. The balmy air may be transformed into the destructive tornado, the refreshing rain and silvery stream may become a desolating flood, the fire that warms and comforts may be changed into a ruinous conflagration.

The Word, our physical constitution, our environment, will

not permit us to forget, that there is "but a step between me and death."

II. WHAT IS DEATH? What is that to which we approach so closely, yet touch it but once? The Word uses the term death to represent three distinct conditions: physical death, or the separation of the soul from God; eternal death, or the condition of the incorrigibly wicked. The text refers to the first of these conditions. What does separation of soul and body imply?

It does not mean annihilation. It is not an end of conscious existence. Nature teaches the indestructibility of matter and that transformation is not annihilation. The Word and reason teach the indestructibility of the soul, and consciousness as an essential quality of intelligent soul-life.

Science says: "When the organs of the body refuse to perform their functions, thus causing a cessation of the phenomenon called life, the ensuing condition is called death." It is plainer and equally accurate to say, "Death is the departure of the soul from the body when the latter ceases to be a fit habitation." The soul is the tenant of the body. The corpse is a vacated tenement.

III. WHAT DOES DEATH MEAN TO ME?

Primarily it means a breaking away from the world with which our physical senses have acquainted us. The things of time must be left behind. The condition into which this separation will introduce us depends on the life we lived in the flesh. A life of sin, of self-indulgence, of sensual gratification, makes death a denial of the only source of pleasure and introduces the soul to a condition of indescribable misery.

A life of purity and sweetness, in which the virtues of Christ are exemplified; a life which issues from a heart illumined by faith in God and directed by a sacred regard for His Word; such a life rests on the border of God's eternal Kingdom, under the reflected light of the glory world. It lives with, in, and for God, and death is but the gateway to the full day of eternal life.

Life after Death

"If a man die, shall he live again?" — Job 14:14

This is an ancient question. It has been discussed in all ages of human history, by the devotees of every form of religion, and by the teachers of every system of science. Some, like Socrates, the Philosopher, aided solely by the light of nature and human reason, have had some apprehensions of a life beyond; but it remained for Jesus Christ, the Son of God, to bring "life and immortality to light through the gospel," and to give mankind the full assurance of existence after death. There are occasions on which the question may still be profitably considered.

I. *Nature and reason indicate an affirmative answer.*

1. Man, though the highest order of earthly life, is outlived by lower animals. Birds have been known to live one hundred years, and elephants, it is said, may live five hundred. It is not reasonable to suppose that the Creator would have allotted to man, possessing such superior intellectual and moral faculties, an earthly existence comparatively so brief and uncertain, if death ended all.

2. Man has the knowledge and fear of death. The beast has no knowledge of death, and only an instinctive fear of pain or capture. God is good, and He gives a remedy for every natural sorrow. He has not designed to increase our sorrows beyond those of the beasts, by giving us superior knowledge, without also giving a compensation in the hope of a happy immortality.

3. Man has the desire for immortality. The beast has not. God has made provision for the gratification of legitimate desires, as those for food, drink, knowledge, and happiness; and it is reasonable to infer that ample provision is likewise made for the gratification of the desire for life beyond the grave.

4. Man has a desire for perfection which is not fully gratified in this life. Few reach the degree of physical perfection which they covet, possibly none are fully satisfied with their intellectual attainments, and the best of men often

express a desire for greater Spiritual accomplishments. Immortality alone offers the hope of a satisfactory realization of human perfection.

5. Man has almost universally, an expectation of immortality. The belief in an existence after death prevails, practically, among all races of men, civilized and uncivilized. History and tradition indicate that it has generally prevailed from the very beginning of the race. The idea of immortality seems to be innate. God would not have planted the belief so universally in the heart of man, if the fact was not to be realized.

II. *Revelation confirms the affirmative answer.*

God "will render to every man according to his deeds; to them who by patient continuance in well doing seek for glory and honor and immortality, eternal life." "This mortal must put on immortality." "I am the resurrection," etc. John 11:25.

The Death of a Child

"The child is not; and I, whither shall I go?" — Gen. 37:30

The plot of Joseph's jealous brethren had succeeded and yet failed. Succeeded in that they had disposed of their troublesome brother; failed in that their very wrath contributed to Joseph's future greatness. Jacob could not thus see, no more could Reuben, who, of all the brethren, had counseled most pacifically. Thus tears of sorrow often blind our eyes to the truth that jealous death, as it steals away the child, only works out, under God, its highest destiny. It is in our *blind* grief that we cry out with Reuben—"The child" etc. It is difficult for the bereaved to see that in calling their child away God has dealt with them in love, but this appears when we consider.

I. THE PURPOSE FOR WHICH THE CHILD LIVED.

1. *To glorify God.* Truly a sweet child with his winsome ways and unclouded life is a glory to God. All of God's creatures are created for some wise purpose. He who can create

anything so lovely as a little child is a beneficent being, and man will learn to glorify him because of these little ones. He also lived

2. *To His parents.* He has made them purer, sweeter, better, more sober, thankful and devout. Parenthood ennobles, and responsibilities pave the way for blessings. Thoughts of the pain, weariness, and anxiety occasioned by the demands of the child are all lost in love. But, He lived

3. *To Himself.* His life was already successful. "Man's chief end is to glorify God and enjoy him forever." This end has the child reached. His purity was a model to all who would be saved. "Except ye become," etc. "For of such," etc. But,

II. FOR WHAT PURPOSE WAS HE TAKEN? Remember that only in an earthy sense "the child is not." He lives, in the hearts of the bereaved and in the presence of God.

1. *He is infinitely blessed now.* Even a child's life has pain. His sorrows are none the less real to him because they do not assail us. Rev. 21 and 22.

2. *He is rescued from Spiritual death.* This is the real terror. Sin is death's sting. For what are you rearing your children? This great question is happily decided for this little one. Is it so decided for *your* children?

His early departure has mellowed the hearts of the bereaved, and teaches them lessons. This is the proper effect of affliction. For the present grevious but glorious in results. Be patient, submissive under, and even grateful for, affliction. Heb. 12:5-11. But consider,

III. THE IMPORTANT QUERY, "And I, whither shall I go?" Notice the condition, spirit and anxiety which such a question implies. We answer—*Go to Jesus, and he* will teach you—

1. *How to follow the child.* He can no more come to you, but you may go to him. Fail not to do it. Make sure, trust not to resolutions, but go at once. Let your new life be as pure and blameless as was that of the child. He will also teach,

2. *Of God's love.* Longfellow's *"The Reaper and the Flowers."* He has bruised your soul to cause it to yield fragrance. Be able to go to the full length with Job 1:21; 13:15.

3. *Of life's character.* Its earthly darkness, uncertainty and brevity, its heavenly brightness, duration and certainty. May it prove true of the bereaved that "a little child shall lead them."

The Death of a Child

"I shall go to him, but he will not return to me."
— II Sam. 12:23

Gone on the returnless journey. Yet safe at home in the Mansions of Heaven. Sweetly at rest in the everlasting arms are those dear ones who die in infancy. Such is the Christian Faith as drawn from the Holy Scriptures in the express teachings of Christ. Of such is the Kingdom of Heaven.

Death is no respector of persons either in age, time, place or condition in me. This unwelcome messenger visits alike the home of royalty as well as that of the humblest citizen. It is here that "the rich and the poor meet together; the Lord is the maker of them all." So too, alike, and for all, are the very many exceeding great and precious promises of God in Christ, as these by Faith reveal to us the all-sustaining "hope of the immortal life beyond;" and also the promise of His gracious presence to guide our steps, to cheer our hearts, to comfort and sustain us amid life's many sorrows and bereavements, which *hope* we have like an anchor to the soul.

1. *Is the child dead? and they said he is dead. Can I bring him back again?* Nay, Father, as seemeth good in thy sight, even so be it unto me. "Not my will but thine be done." Thou gavest, thou hast taken away. Blessed be thy Holy Name.

> "There is a voice that hears,
>   When heaviest weighs Life's galling chain."
> 'Tis Heaven that whispers "Dry thy tears,"
> "The pure in Heaven shall meet again."

2. *I shall go to him, but he will not return to me.* True, oh King, but in what way and through what door? Christ says, I am the way, the truth, the life; I am the door, by Me if any man enter in. These little ones, dying in infancy,

enter Heaven through innocency, purity, truth and loveliness of character; no sin, no actual transgression of God's Holy law. From even the *taint* of a sinful nature cleansed in the precious blood of Christ, saved through the infinity of Christ's atoning sacrifice.

> "Not for the babe that sleepeth there,"
> My tears bestow, my sorrows give —
> Pass on, and weep with grief sincere,
> "For those who innocence outlive."

I shall go to him, but he will not return to me. Yes, dear friends, we may go to meet Christ in Heaven, and with loved ones gone on before in their infantile years. But only as members of the great "Family of the Redeemed," "by the way of the cross," with hearts purified from all sin through repentance and Faith, washed in the blood of Christ, in whom there is redemption from sin.

> " 'My little one, my sweet one,'
> Thou can'st not come to me,
> But nearer draws the numbered hour,
> When I shall go to thee.
> And thou, perchance with Seraph smile,
> And Golden Harp in hand,
> May'st come the first, to welcome me,
> To our Immanuel's Land."
> "Beyond the river."

My Departure

"The time of my departure is at hand." — II Tim. 4:6

An Old Testament saint suffering from a severe affliction which caused him pain day and night, exclaimed—Job 30:23. If at any time we should think of death it is when the tabernacle of our body is made to tremble by the power of disease. Paul too, is contemplating death. He says, "the time of my departure," etc. But how different the circumstances! He was "the prisoner of Jesus Christ," under sentence of death, and the time of his martyrdom was imminent.

I. OBSERVE THE MANNER IN WHICH HE SPEAKS OF DEATH.

1. *A departure.* The Scriptures speak in peculiar language of death in its relation to believers. Called a gathering unto the fathers, sleeping in Jesus, gain, etc. The death of the Christian may appear to be like that of the unregenerate, but there is a difference indescribably great. For all true believers the Son of God has abolished death. II Tim. 1:10. Not that they are exempt from the law of death, Heb. 9:27, but as one has said, "death is so changed with regard to the believer that it does not deserve the name." The text contains a beautiful sentiment. It is said that the Apostle had said, "the time is all but here when I shall go home."

2. *It is imminent.* The time is at hand. There are many within a hands-breadth of the grave, and yet they put far away the day of death. The aged man leans on his staff tottering under the weight of years and they say, "His time is short." A sick friend is the victim of some dangerous malady, and they say with tears in their eyes and sadness in their hearts—"He cannot live till morning." But they little think they may follow *soon.* "John out-runs Peter to the sepulchre, but Peter is not far behind."

II. THE SPIRIT IN WHICH PAUL CONTEMPLATES DEATH. He was evidently waiting in readiness and expectation for his departure. Hence the sublime out-pourings of his soul. Vs. 6-8.

1. *Here is clearly indicated consciousness of preparedness.* His work was finished. His personal salvation stood complete in Jesus. As a servant of the Lord, he was waiting for the time of reckoning. This life is the golden season when salvation may be obtained, and it shall be chiefly employed in this pursuit. Matt. 6:33. Moreover, life is a sacred trust which we are to keep till the Master of the house cometh. Our life is not ours; we are trading with our Lord's money. Matt. 25:14.

2. *Paul's utterances breathe a spirit of blessed expectation.* He thinks of death, it appears, not with regret and fear, but with, "a smile of desire, with a flush of expectancy." His de-

parture would bring him to his Master and a crown of righteousness, and this was something worth going through all the horrors of martyrdom to possess. The day of the Christian's departure is his ascension-day to Paradise, where he shall be crowned with "joy unspeakable and full of glory." Such knowledge not only produces calmness and composure, but joyous anticipation. When sentence of death was pronounced upon Socrates, he said to his judges, "Is this, do you think, no happy journey? Do you think it nothing to speak with Orpheus, Musaeus, Homer and Hesiod?" The Christian's death is a departure to be with Jesus. Such a prospect may well rejoice the heart and give sweet consolation in our last journey.

A Song in the Night

"Behold God is my Salvation. I will trust and not be afraid. . . ." — Isa. 12:2

We find *evanescent* written upon all things terrestial. Like the mirage of the desert, the things which we hope to reach, and which present a fair and beautiful prospect, vanish as we approach, or lead us still further on to despair. Not so with the Christian who reads his credentials, and finds he has a passport from all this scene of uncertainty and disappointment to that glorious Heaven of repose. The reading of the roll given him, produces joy, and he hath given with it a song in the night.

I. THE BLESSED ASSURANCE OF THE CHRISTIAN. It is given to the Christian to be assured that Jesus is his now. It is not presumption to say—"My Beloved is mine and I am his." It is a grasp of the principle of Faith imparted by the Holy Spirit. It is a sweet foretaste of that joy which shall one day be increased. The words of Job, David, Paul, were not presumptious. See Job 19:25; Ps. 19:15; II Tim. 1:12. There are seasons when the soul can say—"God is my Salvation." The mariner that has been tempest-tossed knows how to appreciate the harbor. To enjoy blessed assurance of divine possession we must be much in communion with God.

II. THE TRUST REPOSED.—"*I will trust and not be afraid.*" Assurance of God as our Salvation, of everlasting arms underneath brings trust. Cause for fear is removed by what has been declared. John 10:28. Yet doubts will exist, and we never deal with facts. There are four special things which the Christian fears and from which God is his salvation. (a). *Self.* (b). *Sin.* It mixes with all he does: intrudes into devotions and meditations. (c). *Satan.* He comes with temptations. (d). *Death.* Nature shrinks from the tomb, from dissolution, from the mysterious beyond. Some are all their life-time subject to bondage through fear of death. These are facts which cause fear to arise in the mind. But the language of the text is, "*I will trust and not be afraid.*"

III. THE REASON ASSIGNED.—"*For the Lord Jehovah is my strength,*" etc. The words (a quotation from Ex. 15:2) state the circumstance. Language fails, when we attempt to describe the name Jehovah. In it concentrates all the glorious trinity of the God-head. Herein lies the force of reason for the soul not fearing—This God of Creation, and center of Redemptive scheme, is our God. Notice some great and blessed truths connected with this name, as a reason for trust. 1st. His name is *Jehovah Jireh*—the Lord will provide. All things are His, whether in Kingdom of Nature or Grace. Consider the lillies of the field, and fowl of the air. "Shall He not much more clothe and feed you both in body and soul. Ye of little faith?" "Cast all your care upon Him," etc. 2nd. He is *Jehovah Nissi*—The Lord our Banner. See Ps. 60:4. "God is love." As the banner is elevated to be a signal, so shall the soul be lifted up above all these varied trials and experiences. 3rd. He is also *Jehovah Shalom*—Signifying God of Peace. Paul says—"He is our peace." When fears present themselves remember it; He hath wrought a reconciliation between an offending sinner and an offended God. Isa. 26:3. 4th. He is *Jehovah Shammah*—The Lord is here. Wherever you may be, in whatever state of feeling, whatever trial, whatever sorrow, the Lord is there. Isa. 43:2; Matt. 28:20. 5th. He is *Jehovah*

Tzidekenu — The Lord our Righteousness. The spotless robe of Christ's righteousness covers all my deformity. Arrayed in this you shall life up your head with joy amid flaming worlds. His righteousness accounted as your own. What reason can be had more strong than this for saying with holy confidence.— "God is my Salvation," etc.

IV. THE REPETITION.—*"He also has become my Salvation."* Emphasis must be placed upon this truth, "that there is none other name under Heaven," etc., no other Salvation. Time short for seeking it. Today! Now! All must die and come to the grave. "Thou shalt die and not live." "Be ye ready," etc. Thanks be unto God, who giveth us songs in the night.

A Triumphant Death

"O death where is thy sting? O grave, where is thy victory?"
— I Cor. 15:55-57

Death is a stranger, always has been and always will be. It matters not how often he comes into our family we never recognize him as a friend, he is the common foe of all men, and we may well ask, what is he? Whence came he? Wherein lies his power? How may he be overcome? Death is the dissolution of the body—the separation of the soul from the body—the end of our earthly being—the end of our probation.

I. WHENCE CAME HE?

1. *Sin brought death into the world.* God had not designed that man should die, but had so created him that he could have been eternally happy had he not disobeyed.

2. *Take sin out of the world and you will have Heaven upon earth.* Banish from society all evil doers and this world will be ready for the Millenium Glory.

3. *All nature abhors death.* This is manifest in the lower and higher beings of creation; death acts alike on human and animal nature. There is a "sting" in death for all—a struggle of life for life.

II. WHEREIN IS THE POWER OF DEATH, OR "THE STRENGTH OF SIN?"

1. *It is in "the law."* The law could not exist were it not for sin, and without the law there would be no sin, Rom. 3:20; Rom. 7:7.

2. *Through the power of sin, God is robbed of that which rightfully belongs to him.* God created you for his glory and your happiness, and yet while the soul is under the power of sin it cannot glorify God, neither be happy.

3. *It is within the realm of sin to afflict the body.* Were it nor for sin we would not be subject to all manner of diseases and epidemics.

4. *It reaches beyond the grave,* and has the power to separate from God and eternal blessedness.

III. HOW CAN THE POWER OF SIN AND DEATH BE TAKEN? "By God which giveth us the victory through our Lord Jesus Christ."

1. *The Christian alone knows the secret by which to overcome death.* It is said of him, "though he die, yet shall he live." By faith in Christ he has the principles of eternal life in him.

2. *Christ overcame death and took from death the sting, and from the grave the victory, and what was impossible for the Law Christ did for us; He brought life and immortality to light through His Glorious Resurrection.*

3. *The Christian being united with Christ, can calmly wait for the hour of his departure.*

4. *Death is victory for him. Paul Blumhardt* said while dying, "light breaks in! Hallelujah." *Robert Newton.*—"I am going, going, going to glory! Farewell sin, farewell death!" *Rev. Freehorn Garrettson.*—"Holy, holy, holy, Lord God Almighty! Hallelujah, hallelujah!" *Bp. Wm. McKendree.*—"Tell my friends, that whether for time or eternity, all is well." *Alfred Cookman.*—"I am sweeping through the gates washed in the blood of the Lamb."

To Die Is Gain

"To die is gain." — Phil. 1:21

Paul was a prisoner of Nero and might be expected to feel thus. Life was growing burdensome and friends were few. Incurable sufferers, and those whose heads are bowed down with sorrow might be expected to feel thus. But death is not gain to all. The atheist cannot say this, nor the worldling. To the Christian only "To die is gain."

1. *Because death removes us from all the evils of this present world.* The children of this present world have comparatively few struggles or trials, and the reason is they float with the current. Their treasures are all here below; they love the world and the things of the world. Not so with the Christian. In the word he must have tribulation because the entire course of the world is at variance with a life of faith. The Christian must strive against its false principles and wicked practices, just as a ship at sea must contend against destruction. Offences must come. Those who die in Christ are forever free from the world, the flesh and the devil. Slander, malice, or persecution may play over their graves, but over this barrier they can never pass.

2. *Death is gain to the Christian because it secures unfailing joys.* We associate with the first Adam, everything that is beautiful and lovely. But what is that compared with the Paradise of the Second Adam—the Lord of Heaven? The earthly Canaan was a goodly land; in the midst of it stood the city which was beautiful for situation, the joy of the whole earth, but what were the attractions of the earthly to those of the Heavenly Canaan?

3. *Death is gain to the Christian because it frees him from the possibility of pain and sorrow.* Here the sources are like the stars for multitude. Spirit harps constantly wail out melancholy dirges. Thousands besides Elijah have gone to Heaven in chariots of fire, behind the harnessed steeds of suffering and sorrow. In many homes bloom such trees as the "sorrow tree" of India, whose flowers expand in the night time. Ps. 24:3; Rev. 21:4. In yonder city there is no night, no darkness

no ignorance, sin or misery. Death has been swallowed up in victory.

4. *Death is gain to the Christian because it delivers him from sin.* That accursed thing could creep into the earthly Paradise and poison every source of human happiness, but nothing impure ever enters with the purified soul, the capitol of the universe. Moral evil never scales its walls, or unbars its gates—who but a devil, would not wish to live where there is no sin.

5. *Death is gain because it introduces us into the immediate presence of Christ.* To be with Christ is every where spoken of in Scripture, as only another name for the perfection of happiness. There can be no happiness where Christ is not. To be with Him, that they might behold His glory, was the richest privilege he could offer his disciples; and when he said to the thief on the cross, "This day shalt thou be with me in Paradise;" he promised him the highest honor in his power to give. On earth this fellowship is unsatisfactory.

6. *Death is gain to the Christian because it brings him into the best society and friendships.* There are more holy beings in the celestial city than any arithmetic can number. There we shall have the companionship of angels and saints made perfect. Rom. 8:18.

Shadows and Sunshine

"A little while, and ye shall not see me...." — John 16:16

Dark and heavy are the clouds that hang over us; sad and sorrowful are our hearts. The sun of our life seems to have set behind impenetrable banks of blackness, and we scarce can bring ourselves to look for a single ray of light. The music of the heart is out of concert pitch; the harp is hung upon the willows by the brooks of affliction, and we cannot sing the Lord's song in this strange land of our bereavement. Yes we do need sympathy; we do need some gentle loving hand to lead us out of darkness into light. We do need to see Jesus. We do need to hear his voice speaking across the troubled waters of life saying—"Peace be still."

I. A FALLING SHADOW.

The words of the text were spoken by the "man of sorrows" to a sorrowing company just previous to a sorrowful occasion. Christ was about to be crucified, etc. It was a case of "knowest thou not that the Lord will take away thy master from thy head today?" To such an inquiry they could only respond with Elisha: "Yea, I know it; hold ye your peace." Death is ever at our doors. The sable wings of the grim messenger is forever darkening our bright prospects. Death always brings sorrow; the two are inseparable. Jesus was fully prepared for the terrible ordeal; but the disciples were sad. Death, grave, are words which ever have a solemn sound. Whisperings, soft footsteps, tearful eyes, closed shutters, are accompaniments of this fearful messenger; and there is no beauty in those things that we should desire them, etc.

II. THE SHADOW LIMITED.

Jesus was to be lost to their vision for a brief time. The corn of wheat was to be hid for three days. Afterward they should see it germinate into more abundant life. John 16:22. "A little while," etc. Our sorrows, griefs, bereavements which are the shadows in our lives are limited.

1. They are only severe enough to accomplish God's purpose in us. God is never redundant in his action. Proof of this is in the gift of his Son for your redemption. Could the world have been saved in any other way, it would have been.

2. The shadows are only for a "little while." Christ speaking of the destruction of Jerusalem and the tribulations that should come then says: "But for the Elect's sake whom he has chosen, he hath shortened the days." The Church must pass through persecutions, etc., but God will limit the time of endurance. II Cor. 4:17. The Lord will not try us above what we are able to bear.

III. THE SHADOW DISCIPLES.

As the word is emphatic that they could not see him for a time, so it is just as empathic that they *shall see him*. The Christian is living in the little while of not seeing Christ in person. But Jesus is coming again, then "shall every eye see him." When the diciples saw Christ after his resurrection they rejoiced.

Reflections.—It must be through death, blessings are multiplied to men. John 12:24; John 16:7. So it was in Christ's going and not in his staying that the most beneficent blessings came to the disciples. In the providence of God we are often gainers by losing. God uses these earthly losses of wealth and friends to contribute to our Spiritual welfare. It may be God will give gifts to you and me by this removal. If he should give the Holy Spirit to arouse latent zeal, kindle stronger love, etc., would it not be your gain? It may be expedient that this one go away, ere salvation come to some hearts and homes.

Attractions of Heaven

"I go to prepare a place for you...." — John 14:2, 3

Heaven is not a dream. Neither is it a mere theological conception, nor a metaphysical abstraction; but a glorious reality. The inspired teacher represents Heaven as a real entity—nay, as more than a mere state of existance. Christ comforts his disciples that it is a *place:* "I go to prepare a place for you." Into this place Enoch was "translated," Elijah in the body drove in a chariot of fire. Christ in the body ascended on high. Consider the attractions of Heaven from these several points of view, and "let not your heart be troubled," for there is comfort here.

1. *Heaven is a place fully prepared.* "I go to prepare a place for you"—Not that the place did not exist before, for it is "the Kingdom prepared for you from the foundation of the world"—but Heaven, without the personal presence of Christ, was not fully prepared for his people. What is a home

when loved ones are absent. So it is with Heaven without the personal presence of Jesus. His presence is essential to the completeness of that place—"and receive you unto myself." With Jesus there, it lacks nothing."All things are now ready," since "the fore-runner is for us entered" to receive his own. It is a "purchased possession," fully paid for, and eminently adapted to the comfort of his people. How different is Heaven in this respect from our best early homes? Our earthly home is not so finished and complete.

2. *Heaven is a place forever permanent.* A home "which fadeth not away." There are "many mansions" there—not frail tents, or tottering tabernacles, but *permanent* buildings—"A city which hath foundations, whose builder and maker is God." Is your soul not drawn in that direction by the force of such a consideration? Ah! yes: the Christian heart longs for home, a *permanent* home.

3. *Heaven is a place exquisitely pleasant.* Nothing will be there to mar the happiness of any—"Nothing that defileth, neither worketh abomination." But the glory and honor of the nations"—the very *Elite* of the universe will be there. Note,

1. *Its society will be the most congenial.* (*a*) *Christ* will be the saint's chief joy. Paul's highest ideal of heaven's pleasures: "To depart and be *with Christ*."—John's highest conception of the glories: "We shall *be like him*." (*b*) *Holy Angels* will be our companions. How sweet such association! (*c*) *Departed friends will be there to greet us.* This is no mere fancy. Jesus taught it as an inducement to us—"And shall sit down with Abraham, Isaac and Jacob," etc.

2. Its *peace* will be most sweet—"A rest to the people of God."

3. *Its employment will be the most delightful.* There will be no more drudgery in the service of God—langor or indifference—no more lukewarmness, or coldness.

4. *Heaven is a place absolutely perfect.* No such perfection here. But we are taught to look for the time "when that which is perfect is come." 1. We shall be *perfect bodily.*—I Cor. 15: 41-44—No more sickness, etc. We shall awake in his likeness. 2. We shall be *perfect mentally*—I Cor. 13:9-12. 3. We shall be

perfect morally.—I Pet. 1:4; Rev. 21:27. How attractive then! Are the leadings of your heart not in that direction? Do you not want to go?

No Night There

"There shall be no night there." — Rev. 22:1

In the first chapter of the Bible we have an authentic, inspired account of the origin of the universe. The first verse of that remarkable chapter satisfactorily answers the profound questions of science and philosophy—questions which are forever utterly inexplicable except on the assumption and statement of that verse which is a very sun-burst upon the midnight of our ignorance. But our admiration for the superior character and contents of this blessed Book, only increases as we come to these closing chapters, and behold the gates of the Heavenly Jerusalem standing invitingly open to the blood-washed of every nation and tongue under Heaven. The strongest figures are employed to indicate to us the future abode and bliss of the saved; but all these doubtless come far short of the actual—types only of an indescribable antetype. Yet much positive information comes to us through the negative description of the text. Our text is a rift in the apocalyptic cloud that over-hangs the eternal future, ere life and immortality are brought to light.

1. Night is an emblem of ignorance. In this world our knowledge is only elementary. After all the boasted acquisitions of modern science, still verily

> "We grope as those in darkened ways
> Thro all that is existant."

What little we see is "through a glass darkly," and what little we know, we know only "in part." But to us who fear God, there is another world and a life to come, a life under vastly improved conditions. There, delivered from the painful limitations of this prison life, we shall "know even as we are known." What if nature denies to the patient research of the devout students many profound secrets? What if God in providence "moves in a mysterious way?" To us is the assurance that "what thou knowest not now thou shalt know hereafter."

2. Night is an emblem of insecurity. The tide of depraved conduct rises at night-fall. The dishonest and murderous purpose is executed under cover of darkness; then life and property are most endangered. But in the glowing splendor of Heaven's perpetual day we shall have the most absolute security.

3. Night is emblematical of evil. Sin is a night-shade. It is dark in its essence and in the product of its infernal energy. After nearly six thousand years of this awful moral eclipse, which has chilled, blighted and dwarfed everything here, it is cheering to know that just ahead is a land where comes no night.

4. Night is an emblem of sorrow. In the name of our common humanity, the poet sadly sang:

> "Thro sorrow's night and danger's path,
> Amid the deepening gloom,
> We, followers of our suffering Lord,
> Are marching to the tomb."

And if sometimes the sorrowing saint mourns even an absent Lord, it is assuring to know that "The clouds and darkness are round about Him, righteousness and judgment are the habitation of His throne." "Weeping may endure for a night, but joy cometh in the morning."

5. Night is an emblem of death. Death reigns here; but Jesus victoriously contested His domination and is for all His people the resurrection and the life. The sun of our life does not set in death, but o'er life's wreck rises to its kindred sky. Beyond this cloud-land of Plutonian night dawns Heaven's eternal day.

Preparation for Death

"Thus saith the Lord, set thine house in order...." — Isa. 38:1

The object of a funeral service is not to improve the condition of the departed Spirit, for this is impossible. What we

could do for the soul should be done in life, and there is no
foundation in Scripture for praying for the dead. Pray for
your friends and neighbors while they are well. Neither is it to
inform the friends and the surviving neighbors where the
Spirit has gone, for in this we are liable to be mistaken, save
in the case of the children. But one object of funeral services,
is to pay respect to the body and give to the mortal remains
of our departed kindred a Christian burial; for this is the
last tribute of respect that can be shown to these earthly
tenements. We love our bodies—the partners with us of our
joys and sorrows. Though our burial will not affect our spiritual condition or eternal destiny, and though we look for a
glorious resurrection, yet we desire to be buried with Christian honors, not like a heathen or a brute. Infidels bury their
dead like "the dumb, driven cattle," and there is not a soli-
tary song in the literature of infidelity to cheer the heart of
a dying man. The Christian can sing:
                    "O come, angel band," etc.

Another object of funeral services is to impress the lessons
of mortality upon the hearts of the living. Men are prone to
forget the stern truth *that they must die.* While absorbed in
the things of time and sense, engrossed with the cares and
business of this world, it is necessary to have the verities of
the eternal world emphasized. Hence the lesson of the text:

1. "THOU SHALT DIE."—*Thou,* individually—none can
ward off the grim monster. None can evade his cold and icy
grasp. Every one of us must succumb to the inevitable decree.
Shalt, it is certain, in fact the only positive and certain event
of the future. None can escape. The high, the low, the rich,
the poor, the noble and the ignoble, must yield to the sway of
death's sceptre. He is no respector of persons, but comes to
all ranks and stations of life, irrespective of taste or wealth,
regardless of the ties of affection that unite the loving hearts
of kindred.

II. "Therefore, in view of this, "SET THINE HOUSE IN ORDER."

1. Set your house in order *temporally.* Have your business
and temporal affairs in a proper shape.

2. Set your house in order *Spiritually*. Attend to the religious instruction of your children. A legacy better than millions is a parent's goldy example and holy training. If your children are not converted under your roof, where can you expect them to be saved?

3. Set your *soul* in order. Disordered by sin—affections, desires and motives awfully out of order. Prepare your house for the *last visitor*.

The Death of Our Little Ones

"My beloved is gone down into his garden ... to gather lilies."
— Sol. Song 6:2

1. Notice the relation of Christ to the Church. "Me beloved," husband and wife.—verse 3.

2. His visits,—"gone down." The plan of salvation. Providences.

3. His "garden."—Figurative of the Church.—A chosen, select people.—"I have chosen you."

I. "Gather *lilies*." The lily proper, a large family.

1. The white lily, an emblem of purity. For beauty, grace and fragrance, is not excelled. Very much like our *little ones*. (a) Beauty,—white, pure and precious. What a part they have in the pleasures and joys of life, they adorn the home and the church—Type of the true Christian. Matt., 18:3. (b) Grace,—agreeable, mild and forgiving. Who does not admire the lily? Let none despise the children. Matt. 18:6-10. (c) Fragrance,—the sweet odor of the lily perfumes the whole room. The childless home is cheerless, and barren of all those pure and holy affections which they inspire, and draw forth.

2. They may be a blessing.—Matt. 18:5.

3. They are in the "garden" (church), by Christ's atonement—dying in infancy they are saved. Why not if they remain?

4. Like the lily is watered, etc., so teach early faith in Jesus Christ, and the children will remain in the church. And when

death comes, in youth or old age, it will be true still, "My beloved is gone down into *his* garden to gather lilies," beautiful and fragrant.—Prov. 22:6.

5. He gathers them because he loves them.—Matt. 19:14, 15; Zech. 8:5.

6. Though death is an enemy; The children and saints are ushered into the presence of the *beloved, who* takes them up. —Is. 40:11.

The Fearfulness of Death

"It shall bring him to the King of Terrors." — Job 18:14
"The last enemy that shall be destroyed is death." — I Cor. 15:26

"Death!" A word of five letters! It is monosyllabic! How easily it is pronounced! It only requires a little puff of the breath—a single articulate sound! Yet, what an oceanic word it is! Who can sound its depth; who measure its coast line! What mariner can navigate this awful sea, braving all the way to a desired Haven, its storms, tides and counter-currents!

"Death!" Hearken, O ye sons of mortality, to this most volcanic word in all our language! I pronounce it solemnly! I bate my breath; I hush my own Spirit; I remove the shoes from my feet—for this place seems awful; seems holy—death is here! The poets have called death the "Black Giant;" the "Destroying Angel;" the "Gate of Darkness." The Bible speaks of it as the "King of Terrors;" the "Wages of Sin;" the "Last Enemy!" O what Epithets, coined by man, inspired and uninspired, to give some adequate expression of death! Not as technical terms of the rhetorician do the Bible and the poets use such Epithets, but as actually descriptive of what death is! The Black Giant; the King of Terrors; the Gate of Darkness; the Last Enemy—surely death is all these! Behold the scourge of War; the scourge of Pestilence; of Epidemic; Earthquake; Flood; Hurricane, Cyclone! These are all involved in death— they mean death in all its terrors, blackness and darkness! The world, with its vale of tears, cares, troubles and fears, is in-

volved in death! Eternity is involved in it—the destiny of both
soul and body!

> Eternity! Eternity!
> How long art thou, Eternity!
> O man, full oft thy thoughts should dwell,
> Upon the pains of Sin and Hell,
> Ponder, O man, Eternity!

O what frightful words to put into juxta-position: "Man";
"Sin"; "Death"; "Hell"; "Eternity"! They make the nerves
tingle; the brain shudder, and the heart strings quiver! O
may they do more than simply effect us physically and mentally. May they thunder against the Castle Gates of our immortal
souls, until, terrified by the awful tumult and stirred in the
depths of our sinful hearts by their commotion, we may think
of the Lord Jesus Christ who came here to destroy Sin, Death
and Hell; and cry unto Him for mercy—cry with all the
vehemence of the wild Eagle, battered and injured by the
storm in his aeriel flight, crying for a place of refuge!

A man will die for want of air in five minutes—the suffering, while it lasts, is said to be terrible. For want of sleep in
about ten days—the whole brain and nervous system seems to
be on fire, so that the poor victim is, as it were, consumed. In
a week's time, he will die for want of water. The agony of
such a death is beyond all description. From two to five weeks,
a man will die for want of food. No language can depict the
black horrors of starvation in its final stage. Without the
Grace of God, a man will, in a few days, weeks or years, die;
and O the indiscribable agony and horror of that death! We
read that is is a death of "indignation and wrath, tribulation
and anguish," that it is "outer darkness," where there is weeping and gnashing of teeth;" that it is "everlasting burning,"
"a lake of fire and brimstone;" "suffering the vengence of
eternal fire!" In all these instances behold Death riding forth
as the King of Terrors—as an Angel of Destruction piercing
every heart with his awful sword—as the Gate of Darkness
slamming shut upon the poor soul entering the realm where
light is not and from which all peace and hope have forever

departed—as the Wages of Sin; the recompense which a man receives for living in this world without God!

"Death!" O man, I beseech you to contemplate death as your enemy, and destroyer—yea, as the Black Giant of eternal wrath to your soul! Out of Christ, this is what death is to every man! In Him we all can have the glorious victory. The last enemy that shall be destroyed is death.

The Shunammite and Her Child

"Is it well with the child? And she answered: It is well."
— II Kings 4:26

Victory to Faith! Unspeakable joy springing out of a living hope in God! Peace to the sorrowing soul that can say: "It is well!" Crowned with glory are all they who, in the fires of adversity, give glory to the Lord!

The story of the Shunammite is to all parents sorrowing the death of little children, one of the most pathetic and consoling incidents in the Bible. It is a narative of divine compassion and power.

Treatment: (1) The child (8-17); (2) The child's death (18-20); (3) The child's mother (21-30); (4). The child raised from the dead (31-37).

I. THE CHILD. (a) He was a special gift of God. He came into the childless home to be a present joy. Though they had wealth, it took this little one to fill the vacancy. (*b*) Perhaps this mother had some great burden to bear; hence to engage her thought and to fill her home with sunlight and help her to bear more joyously her cross this little jewel of Heaven was dropped into her bosom! (*c*) So it is that often a child, coming into the family in a time of loneliness or sorrow, becomes an unspeakable blessing and demonstrates, beyond all doubt, that it is a special gift of God. (*d*) How some of us are able to thank the Lord daily for the child born to us when our lives were a great tear and our pathway all darkness!

II. THE CHILD DEAD. We short-sighted mortals can see

no reason for this. Why give the poor mother a child, if in a brief while, she must be parted with? Answer (1) We cannot understand the ways of providence. (2) Happiness is only one means by which God seeks to make us better; sorrow is another. (3) It was better for her to have the child a little while than not at all. (4) Brief missions are often the most effective, *e.g.*, John the Baptist and our Lord. It may be the intention that our children's work shall be intense in compass, but brief in duration. (5) Though we may be able to give no reason for this child's death, yet we know that the Mother's Spirit could only be right when able to say in her affliction: "It is well." The test in our sorrow is this, whether or not we can say: "The Lord gave," etc. Job 1:21.

III. THE CHILD'S MOTHER. *(a)* The sword of bereavement pierced her heart. *(b)* In her sorrow she thinks of and goes to the man of God (21-30). *(c)* Of God we should think; to God we should go; in God we should trust; and from God we should seek consolation in times of great sorrow. *(d)* In her affliction she had not one word of complaint. (v. 26). *(e)* She acted with haste (v. 24). (f) In presenting her case to the Prophet she was most earnest (v. 27). (g) She would not trust her cause to Gahazi, only to Elisha—not to man, but to Jesus only. *(h)* Bear in mind that one of the purposes of history is to show us how great men and women have acted on great occasions. Here was a great occasion of sorrow; behold what the heart-broken mother did. Let all in her condition go and do likewise!

IV. THE CHILD RAISED FROM THE DEAD. *(a)* We must not look for the fulfilment of the same thing in our experience. The age of such miracles is past. *(b)* It is probable the Shunammite did not expect her child to be raised to life again. In her sorrow, she went to God, knowing that in his own way he would bless her. *(c)* When she grasped her living child (v. 37), perhaps she said in her heart: *"This is more than I expected."* *(d)* Let us go to God as this woman did, and He will give us the blessing *we most need!* *(e)* The blessing given will eventually be as surprising in its goodness and power as if our dead were restored to life again!

Death the Gift of God

"He giveth his beloved sleep." — Ps. 127:2

Throughout the Old Testament Scriptures especially, *"sleep"* is often put for death. "He slept with his fathers," is a common expression in the Jewish Scriptures. To "sleep in Jesus," is a common way of speaking of those who die in the faith of the Redeemer. We shall take the "sleep," in the text as denoting death and confine our remarks to an illustration of the passage under this one point of view: "surely He giveth His beloved sleep." Let us consider:

I. THE DIVINE SOURCE OF THE GIFT. The Lord is the speaker in the beautiful passage before us. God does not only send the sleep, but He brings it Himself, and lays it on the eyes of His beloved ones. This gift of God is distinguished.

1. *For its kindness and tenderness.* The metaphor takes away the pain of the righteous in the dying hour, and breathes a sweet perfume when spoken over their graves.

2. *For its quietness and peacefulness.* It is solid, and not merely ideal; and is always suitable to the state and circumstances of his saints.—Peter in prison.

3. *For its certainty.* God can never forget His saints. Their every tear is treasured up in God's bottle.

II. DEATH WITH ALL ITS ACCOMPANIMENTS IS BUT JOY TO THE SAINT SINCE IT IS A PART OF HIS INHERITANCE. 1. God Himself stands almost visibly at his side, and his last resting place He will shadow with His wings. His last sickness may be protracted and painful, but nothing in all this struggle, nothing in all this apparent defeat can harm the saint of God. 2. The chamber of the dying saint is crowded with glorious friends. Angels are waiting there to take charge of the soul. A hand gentler than any human is closing those eyes; a voice sweeter than a mother's is whispering, "The Lord giveth His beloved sleep." 3. Ye mourning ones, I know of no greater comfort than the words of the text. What is bestowed by God as a "gift on His beloved" will assuredly occupy His care. His watchfulness, His solicitude; and He will set His zeal, and plant His guardianship where His beloved lie sweetly at rest. Dry your tears and let your faith do its part; because herein God answers your prayer, herein God fulfills His promise. "Blessed be the name of the Lord."

III. THIS HEBREW FORMULA FOR DEATH CALLED "SLEEP" IMPLIES A HAPPY AWAKING AT THE LAST DAY. 1. A happy awaking depends upon the state of sleep, of body and of mind, and upon earnest and faithful work done in the vineyard of the Lord. 2. The nature of this happy awaking: with the likeness of the glorified Savior. We shall be like him both in our new resurrection, body and soul. Everything assimilates to what it is conversant with. The saint has been "looking unto Jesus the author and finisher of his faith." 3. The glorious sight which on awakening we shall first behold. The first sight that greets the waking life must be the wakener. The great wakener is Jesus. Lazarus, when he came forth, saw first the face of him who said, "Lazarus, come forth."

Raised in Power

"It is sown in weakness, it is raised in power." — I Cor. 15:43

The question relative to the literal resurrection of the matter of which the human body is composed may be of interest, but is of less practical importance than many others. The body is to be changed. "It is sown a natural body, it is raised a Spiritual body." Whatever the nature of the bodily change may be, it will not effect the indentity of physical composition. Physiologists teach that in life the body is constantly changing its material; that in seven years every particle of matter contained in it is displaced by another. The person, however, remains the same individual. The story of Enoch Arden and his family, immortalized by the poet Tennyson, and that of Evangeline and her lover, by Longfellow, afford illustration. In the resurrection, "we shall all be changed," but the same persons whom we knew and loved in this life will be raised for the life beyond. The terrestrial body will be replaced by the celestial. The text suggests the idea of:

I. POWER OVER THE NATURAL WEAKNESS OF FLESH AND BLOOD. Immortality would not be desirable in our present condition. When "raised in power" physical weakness will be unknown.

1. *Hunger and thirst.* Many toil from morn till night, year after year, to keep the "wolf from the door." Rev. 7:16.

2. *Weariness.* We are retarded in our earthly pursuits by the necessity of rest. On earth, night is a blessing, for it affords the essential undisturbed repose. Rev. 21:25.

3. *Pain.* Suffering caused by sickness and injury is the common and inevitable earthly lot of man. Rev. 21:4.

4. *Deformity and mutilation.* There will be no empty sleeves, artificial limbs, scarred or misshapen forms, the results of disease and accident, in that celestial land of beauty and perpeutal youth. Phil. 3:21.

II. POWER OVER THE NATURAL WEAKNESS OF THE ORGANS OF SENSE AND OF COMMUNICATION. Life often seems almost a burden to the aged on account of the failure of sight, hearing and speech. When "raised in power," these faculties will not fail.

1. *The eye*—a delicate organ—easily injured. At best it often needs the assistance of the microscope, the telescope, or the smoked glass. After the resurrection, artificial apparatus will not be necessary in order to behold the great and wonderful works of God.

2. *The ear.* Deafness, at least to some degree, is a very common earthly infirmity. The employments of Heaven will largely be musical. The happiness of the saints will not be limited by imperfections of hearing.

3. *The voice.* On earth, some can not speak and many cannot sing. In Heaven, all will their loosened tongues employ." Rev. 15:3.

III. POWER OVER THE NATURAL WEAKESS OF THE INTELLECTUAL FACULTIES. I Cor. 13:12.

1. The power to acquire knowledge will be increased. We are limited now, in the acquisition of knowledge by the imperfection of the organs of sense. When the eye, the ear, and all other organs of apprehension are "raised in power," the ability to know will evidently be greatly augmented.

2. The power to retain knowledge will be increased. A common and very perplexing mental infirmity is a defective memory. The mind holds latent knowledge which ordinarily can not be utilized. Doubtless, when "raised in power," the ability to retain and to recall will be wonderfully improved.

3. The opportunities to gain knowledge will be increased Our ability to acquire knowledge depends upon the adaptation of our faculties to the resources of knowledge at hand. On earth, the adjustment is not perfect. In Heaven, "when that which is perfect is come," by a superior correspondence of things, facilities for understanding and knowledge will, doubtless be realized which here and now none can comprehend.

The Blessed Encomium

"Well done, good and faithful servant.... — Matt. 25:21

In this chapter St. Matthew reports two of the parables of our Lord. The parable of the ten virgins and the parable of the talents. The first parable instructs us *regarding our duty to ourselves*. We owe it to ourselves to make necessary preparation for death, judgment and eternity. We should do as the wise virgins did, and not follow in the foosteps of the foolish virgins. We must ground our hope for heaven and eternal bliss not on mere forms of religion, but see to it that we are well supplied with the oil of experimental religion and saving grace. The second parable instructs us *regarding our duty to God*. We owe it to God that we prove ourselves faithful servants in the discharge of the trusts committed to our care. We should imitate those two servants who traded with the talents entrusted to them, and thereby doubled their value. We must not follow the example of the third servant who hid the talent

committed to his care in the earth. Should we do as this slothful servant did, then in the day of final reckoning the righteous
Judge will have to denounce us in these terrible words: "Thou
wicked and slothful servant!" May we rather so love and live,
do and dare in the service of God, that at the close of life's
day we may hear from the lips of the kind Master the touching
encomium: "Well done, good and faithful servant!" Observe

I. THE PRAISE WHICH THE LORD BESTOWS ON
THE FAITHFUL SERVANT.

1. *The Lord commends him as a servant.* The Christian
was once a servant of sin and unrighteousness. Receiving by
faith the redemption in Jesus, he was released from this terrible bondage, and became the servant of God and righteousness. Rom. 6:17, 18. He is serving an unseen Master. The
Christian is not to be a mere ornament in the church, like
those silver statues in one of the great churches in England
during the days of Oliver Cromwell. Being told that these
represented the twelve apostles, he sternly exclaimed: "The
twelve apostles are they? Well take them away at once, and
melt them down and coin them into money that, like their
Master, they may go about doing good." Every Believer is to
go about doing good; he is not to be passive, but active in
regard to God's work.

2. *The Lord commends him as a good servant.* He gives
him a testimonial of good character. To do good we must be
good. We cannot perform any good works, unless we are
created unto them in Christ Jesus. Hence good works are the
evidence of the renewal of our nature. Only the good tree will
habitually bring forth good fruit. As the body is to the soul,
so are our deeds to the heart out of which they spring. Our
deeds are the body in which our hearts and desires clothe
and manifest themselves.

3. *The Lord commends him as a faithful servant.* "Thou
hast been faithful over a few things." Faithfulness is the duty
which this parable inculcates. Not the acquisition, but the
fidelity is commended and receives the encomium of the Lord.
Faithful discharge of their duties is that which God requires

of his stewards. All human life is sacred stewardship. Stewardship implies responsibility; responsibility requires fidelity. In
all the positions and relationships of life our faithfulness is
being tested. Let us be loyal to God, to conscience, to the
eternal principles of truth and righteousness. Let us always
and in everything be faithful.

II. THE REWARD WHICH THE LORD GRANTS TO
THE FAITHFUL SERVANT.

1. *The Lord confers higher honors upon him.* "I will make
thee ruler over many things." A man proves himself fit to go
higher, who shows that he is faithful where he is. An individual that will not do well in the present position, because
he or she longs for a higher place, is neither fit for the present
nor a higher position. Such a person is too high already and
should be put lower. Now Jesus has declared, "If any man
serve me, him will my father honor." Having been true and
loyal in the lower station of this life, they shall be promoted
to a higher station in the life to come. Having confessed Jesus
before men, He will confess them before His Father and the
Angels. They shall be kings and priests unto God and the
Lamb forever. They shall bear palms of victory in their
hands and crowns of glory upon their heads.

2. *The Lord grants him admittance into everlasting joy.*
"Enter thou into the joy of thy Lord." This world is fre-
quently called a "vale of tears." There are tears enough
shed here to prove, most assuredly, the truthfulness of this
designation. However, we can with still greater truthfulness
designate heaven "a land of never ending joy and bliss." It
will be the joy of eternal victory, the joy of perfect safety.

My Change

"My change." — Job 14:14

We live in a world of changes. Many of them are expected but dreaded, while others come as welcome, because

of hopes connected with them. The earth, with all the world about us, rests us from one condition of things by changing to another before monotony sets in. "Chance and change are busy ever." In our family life these changes come. We move from one locality to another, from one business to another, some children leave the paternal roof and form new homes, and all is fraught with risk and uncertainty amidst feelings of mingled doubt and hope. Many, particularly the aged, hesitate to make changes because of the strong element of uncertainty that is ever manifested.

Job's life was so full of pain, of unrest, of unhappy memories—the same monotonous misery day after day—that he was compelled to look longingly for death as a deliverer. Death presents itself to us in varied aspects: sometimes dreaded as the opening to an unseen world of misery; again greeted as the angel of real life to the Christian it means home, rest, heaven.

To Job the grandest aim was that of a change—and almost any change would have been welcome. Death is a change of worlds to all of us. It is a settler of destinies. It opens the portals to life or to the second death. It is a change of employments, of loves, of companionships. The family life, the grandest institution of earth, is given up because its work is done and we enter into the heavenly brotherhood of all God's children.

Although Job called death a change, he looked at it in another light, for he asked that question propounded by all humanity: "If a man die shall he live again?" No doubt he had a belief in immortality, but that belief was beclouded in the uncertainties of his day. Nevertheless he was willing implicitly to trust his God.

Crito asked Socrates, after he had taken the cup of poison, what disposition should be made of him after he died, to which Socrates replied: "You may bury me if you can catch me." In this statement he revealed a rational faith in immortality far transcending the age in which he lived. But, like Job, he lived without the evidences that have come down to us. That question, "If a man die shall he live again?" for centuries unanswered, meets reply in the condescension of God himself, and all the uncertainty is taken away by the personal assurance of Jesus that "he that believeth in me, though he were dead, yet shall he live." John 11:25. Job's question is *shall he live?* Christ's positive answer is, *he shall.*

While eternal existence is the lot of all men, the state of that existence, whether of happiness or of misery, is conditioned: "He that *believeth* in me . . . shall . . . live.

Job waited for his "change" but he waited with his heart prepared to meet his God. May we redeem the time and await His coming in faith's assurance that all will be well.

Our Sainted Dead: They Are Living Epistles

"Ye are our Epistle." — II Cor. 3:2

It was no fancy of Chrysostom when he said: "The true Shechinah is man." He could not have meant that every man is the true Shechinah of God. The wicked reveal the darkness of Satan and not the glory of Heaven. Of course this is the meaning: The true representative of God on earth is the sincere Christian. "We witness" says the author of Ecce Deus, "and are daily called upon to read ever-enlarging editions of the New Testament, in the lives and characters of God's children." Even Paul could say to the members of the church at Corinth: "Ye are our Epistles," etc. II Cor. 3:2, 3.

In our Lord's own ministry, we behold Him recognizing the Christian to be His own *Open Epistle,* written by His Spirit, and revealing His goodness and love. As an example of this, see the humble obscure woman of Bethany, who poured upon His head the precious ointment; and of whom Christ said: "Wheresoever this Gospel" etc. Matt. 26:13.

The act performed demonstrated the divine principle that was in Mary—revealed the real Christ Spirit she possessed. It was the Schechinah, not in an effulgent cloud, but in sweet, loving, self-sacrificing life! Her use of the alabaster box showed her to be a living Epistle. Jesus had written it, not with ink, but with the Spirit of the living God. And this is what Jesus is always doing: Writing enlarged editions of the Gospel with the pen of the Holy Ghost upon tables that are hearts of flesh.

Our Sainted Dead, who lived here in trust and love and who have left behind them years of toil for the Master, are, today, "Living Epistles!" In their lives, those of us who knew them, can read the great Gospel in all its power, and contemplate Jesus in His beauty, simplicity and love, as He has lived, in our own homes, churches and neighborhoods! While here in the flesh they represented God—were the "true Shechinah"—real Epistles of Life! Death has not changed them. It has only made them more perfect.

To the bereaved and sorrowing, these "Living Epistles" are a glorious source of consolation. (1) In the fact that they have gone to their rich reward. (2) Death, instead of destroying the living characters of grace and truth in their souls, has only made them more glorious, so that we, still living, are able to read these jewelled pages in clearer light and with greater profit to our own souls. What truly faithful servant of Christ—Mother, Father, Pastor, Friend, Philanthropist, Statesman—has not been blessed to the home, church or land, long after life's career has been ended! What a consolation it is for us to have, that though our sainted dead are not with us, they yet live—live as Epistles of Light to be daily read! (3) These Epistles, often being more easily comprehended than the written word itself, are correspondingly powerful in preparing us for their companionship above. (4) We see in such Living Epistles, which the world can not gainsay, the very best evidence of the power of the Cross—the love and goodness by which the ever-living Savior is seeking to still the world's selfishness; wipe away its tears of grief; and make beautiful, and glorious every believing soul.

O that we may all so live that we may be, after we have

passed from the stage of action, written Epistles for Christ
known and read by all men?

Christ the Lord of the Dead

"No man dieth to himself." — Rom. 14:7

No star could drop out of its orbit and not effect the entire
stellar universe. No flower can decay and not have an influence on other vegetation. So also is it in the higher realm
of existence—in the kingdom of human being. No man, be
he beggar, criminal, philosopher, king, liveth or dieth to
himself.

The fact showeth the unity of the race; the strong grasp
others have on us and the tension we are all sustaining in
this life—a tension which will give others a shock when once
it has been snapped by our demise. Paul is, however, less
general in his application of this truth: "No man dieth to
himself." He does not mean all men, but only Christians.
This is clearly stated in verses 8 and 9. Read also I Cor.
6:19, 20. Christ is our Owner, Master, Lord, and hence our
Manager, Provider and Care-taker, both in life and death;
hence, every Christian dies unto Christ, because He is his
Lord. This being the case, therefore: 1. The *time* of the
Christian's death is arranged and determined by the infinite wisdom of Christ, his Lord. 2. The *place* of his death
is also fixed by Jesus Christ. 3. The *manner* or *cause* of death
is not left to chance, but in the hands of his Divine Owner.
4. The *loneliness* of death shall be taken away by Him who
is his Companion and sure Friend. 5. All *solicitude* shall be
removed from the dying saint by his bountiful Provider.
6. In his death the true servant of Jesus *will live unto greater
usefulness.* All these things may be the Christian's sure hope,
because Christ is the Lord of the righteous dead.

I. He can hope without doubt that the *time* of his death
is fixed by his blessed Savior. (a) We often wonder that
death comes when it does—why children die, why so many

pass away in the full prime of life and usefulness—why the aged live so long, often in pain and suffering? (b) Revelation solves this mystery in the doctrine of the Divine Ownership. Paul said: "The time of my departure is at hand." Who fixed that time—Paul, the Romans, or God?

II. The *place* of the Christian's death is also in the Lord's hand. It often adds to the agony of bereavement that the person died away from home remote from friends, a stranger in a strange land, unknown and unministered to by tender hearts. All this may be added to the grief of the bereaved but infinite wisdom can make no mistake. It was the Lord's purpose.

III. Then, too, the *manner* or *cause* of death is exceedingly perplexing. Great storms carry good people to the bottom of the sea. Some are swept away by floods. Many by strange providences. We wonder that so good a man as Paul should be beheaded; or Hugh Latimer burned to death. The truth before us alone can give us light—Christ, the Lord of the dead. Why then take the believer out of his Owner's hands as to the manner of his exit from this world. In short, if we are Christ's we can cherish the sure hope that the *when* the *where* and the *how* of our death are all determined by infinite wisdom, love and power!

IV. The *loneliness* of death is taken away from the true believer. (a) Loneliness has a terrible power on the human Spirit. How the young and the old have suffered with it. (b) It is associated with death. How often we have heard it spoken of on the death bed. (c) So far as the Christian is concerned, all this is fanciful. He who dies in Christ, to Christ, in order to go to Christ and realize all the fullness of his joy, can not be lonely. (d) The bereaved may be lonely, but not those who pass into glory. They would not come back—their happiness is complete. (e) The lost shall experience all the horror of unspeakable solitude.

V. The truth before us is intended to take away all *solitude* as to our work not being completed; as to those we leave behind us not being cared for and as to every other earthly care. Joseph said: "I die and God will surely visit you." Here we behold the absence of all anxiety about those left behind, etc. God will take care of all. Such is the Christian's faith at death!

VI. To die unto the Lord is to die unto a new and a greater *usefulness.* Heb. 11:4; Rev. 14:13.

Conclusion: From these considerations how glorious it is to live the Christian life and how grand beyond all description to die the Christian's death.

Funeral Sermon

"Seek him that ... turneth the shadow of death into the morning ... The Lord is His name." — Amos 5:8

On the morning after the death messenger made his sad stroke in this peaceful home, how gladly shone the sun! Frowns had fled from nature's visage and only smiles were upon her countenance, the silent rain-tears so long falling, were dried and there seemed a bright prophecy of clearer skies. The night which brought bereavement and grief had closed in with shadows, but He turned them into the morning. Let us hope that life's waning day has also been transformed into the glorious sunlight of immortality.

To the trusting heart death becomes a shadow, a mere spectral illusion through which we must pass, but which cannot harm us. No more can the real monster if we be Christ's. Ps. 23. But who is He by whose power the enemy has been overcome and by whose prowess the grave has been robbed of its victory? He is

I. THE PERSON MENTIONED IN OUR TEXT. "The Lord is His name." The great problem—*Given: Self. To find out: God*—has ever engaged the noblest faculties of the soul. But unassisted creature has never yet apprehended Creator, and so man, despite his lofty philosophies, speculations and analyses, has been unable to reach Him—"the abysmal God." He is

1. *Our Creator.* It is better to be than not to be, although

many have so loathed life as to deprive themselves of it voluntarily. Others, like Saul, have vainly called upon their friends to rid them of their burdensome selves. But such disordered constitutions are, fortunately, in a minority. With what tenacity do we hold to each fleeting moment—as though in its maw it carried away some priceless gem from our store! The pleasure in life comes from upbuilding, the pain from down-tearing—and that results from sin. God is a creator, not a destroyer; a life giver, not a grave maker, therefore to sin must we look as the author of all misery, just as surely as in God we shall find the infinite fountain head "from whom all blessings flow" in copious streams.

2. *Our Preserver.* To create life implies the intention to afford sustenance. The means for our preservation challenge our loving admiration. Think for a moment of God's goodness in that He provides for our wants, natural and cultivated, in so lavish a manner. He in His great love, orders the procession of the equinoxes, the changes of the seasons, the berries to put forth in spring, the vegetables to grow in summer, and the corn to yellow in autumn, while His "cattle upon a thousand hills" are included when He says that all is ours.

3. *Our Savior.* The lessons to be learned from this bereavement all tend toward the cross. God the Son hanging upon the tree a willing oblation for the sins, lapses and shortages of the world becomes to us not a dreamy possibility, or a speculative theory, but a blessed reality thrilling our pulses with a new life—blissful, heavenly! Let the brevity and uncertainty of life, the tremendous weight of personal responsibility, the pressing character of our needs drive us hastily, confidingly to Jesus; upon His mercy let us depend as we rap for admittance at yonder city's portal.

II. AN ASSERTION. "He turneth the shadow of death into the morning." This can the Lord of light right well do. "He covereth Himself with light as with a garment." He rideth on the lightnings. His face is as the sun and His eyes are flames of fire. "All power is given," etc., and by His victory over death and hell He can verify this promise:

1. *Unto the dead.* Life is full of shadows. They begin to gather at the cradle and thicken toward the tomb. With raven wings they attend us life's journey through, their plutonian blackness terrifying our timorous hearts.

2. *For the Bereaved* is this also true. There are few homes in this or any other community over which the shadow of death has not at some time come. Some day He'll disentangle all the knotted threads of this intricate maze of life and His love will lead me out of the shadow into the morning.

3. *To the Sinner.* For you He will turn "the shadow of death into the morning." Think upon your ways, ponder your paths, and ask yourself: Am I not going down into blackness of darkness forever?

III. THE ADMONITION—"Seek Him." I am sure that Amos would advise no one to make any thing but a thorough search after God, for only they that seek earnestly will find Him. Be assured that "it does not take long for an anxious sinner and an anxious Savior to meet." But think not for a moment that these words of earnest admonition are addressed to the sinner alone, they come home to us of the faith as well. Let us all seek him for

1. *This is our clear duty.* To apprehend God is man's chief end.

2. *This is our only help.* The wisdom of this world, helpful as it may be in things pertaining thereto, utterly fails when it is applied to the vast concerns of our souls.

3. *This is our sure life.* In Him is life and it is for all who seek, but they must seek *Him.*

Death at the Door

"There is but one step between me and death." — I Sam. 20:3

Although there is a step, there is but "a step" between you and death. It may be a long or a short one, according to the phraseology here used. The length of a few years in the estimation of God is as nothing: one day with him is as a thousand years, and a thousand years with Him but as one day. He does not compute time as we do, but he computes it with relation to eternity. However any action bears upon eternity that is His reckoning.

What is your life? a handbreadth. What is your life? a vapour which appeareth for a season and then passeth away. What are your days? "swifter than a post" passing like a "weaver's shuttle," as the swift ship upon the ocean. Such my brethren, are the scriptural representations of the life of man.

Besides, the uncertain avenues through which death makes his appearance, render it necessary for every individual to adopt this language. Who expected the flood on the morning that Noah entered the ark? None but Noah and his family.

What seemed less likely than for death to appear on the morning when Lot left Sodom? The sun shone; it was one of the gayest and most beautiful mornings that the earth had ever seen; but just about breakfast time, fire and brimstone descended from Heaven; death rode upon, and carried off the whole population of the city.

It was in the moment of triumph and blasphemy, after daring exploits had been performed by the army, and the whole 185,000 men lay beneath the walls of Jerusalem—that the angel came, waved his hand over them, and slew the whole army in one night.

Herod never felt himself happier than when he stood upon his throne, making a speech to the assembled ambassadors and to the populace around. He was on that day dressed as we are told by Josephus in the most gorgeous robe that eye had ever seen. It was cloth of gold; when the sun shone through the building upon him, he looked more, as the people said, like a god than a man. That was the proudest moment of his existence; the people gave him divine honors. But while they loaded him with all these honors death came, and little worms, which Herod would not have touched, ate up his body and consigned his soul to perdition. Yet there was but a step in all these cases between the individuals and death; and the step was brief and short hurrying these individuals into eternity in a moment.

But is this confined to public life? Public men, engaged in transactions of this kind, are most in danger; but a noble lady of high birth, only a little while ago, was burnt to death in her own mansion; many are drowned in our rivers every year; hundreds of sailors meet a watery grave. How many, by disease which baffles medical aid, are hurried into eternity, in the course of a very short time. And I ask you, my friend, today, in the presence of the mighty Judge, who are you, that you should escape? What assurance have you, that death shall not meet you, as it has done others? Perhaps you are a sinner of no ordinary kind. I may be addressing myself today, to some man who is a drunkard, who is a blasphemer, and I ask that one: What legal bond have you in your own possession that death shall not meet you, and meet you suddenly,—and in the commission of these iniquities, which must hurry every one who is guilty of them into everlasting woe? Oh! my dear friends this text comes to us with immense power—"There is but a step"— but a step "between me and death."

What We Shall Be in Eternity

"Neither can they die any more for they are equal unto the angels...." — Luke 20:36

We are reminded that we live in a world of transition, a world of change, a world where the mutilating hand of time is seen in all things mortal. Today our friends are about us in the freshness and bloom of health, and tomorrow we bend in anguish over their cold forms. But the Savior whose promise it is "to bring life and immortality to light through the gospel" tells us in the text of a land where there is no death. Those who have taken their exit from earth are forever liberated from this invincible conqueror. The light of the gospel of Jesus Christ reveals death to the Christian, as the entrance gateway to eternal life. This blessed doctrine dispels much of the gloom from the grave and gilds the way to heaven with an eternal brightness. Not only are the children of God freed from physical death, but

ARE TO BE "EQUAL TO THE ANGELS."

The contemplation of this thought should fill every disciple of Christ with rapture and delight. If we were able to draw aside the vail that hangs between mortal and immortal beings, and look upon the illustrious intelligences who vie around the eternal throne, we could have a more just conception of what *we are to be.*

1. We are to be equal to the angels in wisdom. "Now we know in part, and prophecy (or preach) in part but then we shall know even also as we are known." We shall then be able "to comprehend with all saints," etc.

2. *As to our habitation and proximity to God.* We are told that "Their angels do always behold the face of the Father." So to be equal to the angels is to enjoy his essential presence which is a state of ineffable delight. "In thy presence is fulness of joy," etc.

3. *As to our employment.* They are God's messengers, sent on missions of mercy or to execute the just judgments of Jehovah. Ps. 103:20, God gave the law from Sinai by the "disposition of angels." Acts 7:53. Heb. 2:2. If God wants to touch a prophet's lips with a "live coal" He dispatches a cherubim to do the work. By an angel He communicates the intelligence to Zechariah of the coming John, and to Mary of Her coming Lord. If God would destroy an oppressing foe, He only has to send one of the grand military cadets of heaven, and one hundred and eighty-five thousand are slain in a single night. An angel brought the tidings of great joy to the shepherds on the plains of Bethlehem. Luke 2:10-13.

4. *Angels are ministering spirits.* Heb. 1:14. Matt. 4:11. Angels visited our Lord on the mount of transfiguration, and were recognized as "Moses and Elias." One of the old prophets came to John in the isle of Patmos. Angels watch over the dying couch of God's children and accompany the

emancipated spirit home to the paradise of God. "The chariots of God are twenty thousand even thousands of angels."
Predicating our argument upon the great truth of the Savior
declared in the text, we are able to infer: 1. That we are to
be infinitely more wise. 2 More happy. 3. In more glorious
employment than it is possible for us to be cumbered as
we are with all the infirmities of the flesh.

Not Death; but Life

"Whether we live therefore, or die, we are the Lord's."
— Rom. 14:8

Says Drummond: "Poetry draws near death only to hover
over it for a moment and withdraw in terror. Philosophy finds
it among the mysteries of being, the one great mystery of
being not." From the time the words, "If thou eatest thereof
thou shalt surely die," were spoken in Eden this solemn word
has been linked with human interest of eternal moment. But
what death is, depends upon what life is. If we are God's
through faith in Christ our life is safe, and our death is
secure. If we are the Lord's in the living hour, there comes
the comforting thought, that we shall be His in the dying
hour. Rom. 14:8, 9.

I. THE TIME IS NOT LEFT TO US.

Let us work as though we were to live forever, and yet so
live as if each day were our last. For we are not prepared to
live till we are prepared to die.

II. WE KNOW NOT WHERE DEATH SHALL MEET
US.

Let us be found in no place where Jesus cannot come. If
we are with Jesus through life, we are assured that we shall
be in the right place just where He wants us when the death-
stroke shall come.

III. NEITHER IS THE MANNER OF OUR DEATH
LEFT FOR US TO CHOOSE.

To the Christian, death is but the highway of Pacific commerce that leads up to the gates of the city of God; whereby heavy travelers who have been faithful to God, enter into a peaceful rest. While we may not have the choice of time, or place, or manner of dying, nevertheless there are certain stations in life, in which we can tarry for awhile, that we may make our way sure from earth to heaven. Nothing can be more illustrative of a man's journey through this world and frequent detentions, than the *railway station.* Railway stations are designed to accommodate all classes of persons. All conceivable classes of mankind are found passing through railway stations. So in the gospel to bless and save men; God made a large and free provision for all; since the fall of man, thousands and millions have accepted Christ.

Through this station of free redemption by the cross, vast numbers have already boarded the trains to the better land. Every railroad station has its peculiar features and surroundings; so there are peculiar experiences in the *moral stations* of every man's life. (a) *Conviction.* Wise is the man that stops at this station. (b) *Repentance.* Bitter may be the experience of those who stop here, for a little time; but his will be like the clouds and tempest just before the sunrise. (c) *Faith in Christ.* Here you behold things of intense interest as you catch the glimpses of the home beyond. (d) *Prayers and communion with God.* (e) *Heaven.* When you board the home train after a long absence, every station you pass is nothing to you. All your thoughts center to that spot when the whistle shall sound and the bell ring to signal the approach to the home station. Do you think the interest and anticipation any less, as the saint passes along the rough places of this sin-cursed world to the end of his journey, his heavenly home? "To live is Christ, to die is gain."

Satisfied with Life

"With long life will I satisfy him, and show him my salvation."
— Psalm 91:16

Many interpretations have been offered of the promise contained in the commandment: "Honor thy father and thy mother," etc. All may not be satisfactory, but, nevertheless, it is evidently true that obedience to all of God's commandments tends to increase the duration of man's life. The promise in the text before us, likewise seems to point to length of days, as well as to satisfaction with life. The promise is to the righteous.

I. UPRIGHTNESS IS CONDUCIVE TO LONGEVITY.

1. The righteous man escapes destructive vices. Thousands of the wicked are annually destroyed by intemperance and other equally fatal habits. Life insurance societies make inquiry in regard to man's morals, for they have learned well that sobriety and virtue increase the probabilities of long life.

2. The pious are most likely to avoid the injurious customs of fashionable society. Excess in food, injudiciousness in dress, prodigality in amusement, and dissipation of energy, undermine many constitutions and shorten many lives.

3. Godliness induces tranquility of mind and soul. Anger, fear and hatred consume vitality, while peace, assurance and love promote health and long life.

II. THE UPRIGHT MAN IS SATISFIED WITH THE LENGTH OF HIS LIFE.

1. Many wicked persons desire to live forever. They fear death and desire to escape the inevitable as long as possible. The good man, being prepared to die, is satisfied with whatever number of days he may be permitted to enjoy in the earthly service of his Master.

2. To some the calamities of life are unendurable and they terminate their miserable existence. The man of Faith in God, being sustained by Him who has promised to be "a very present help in trouble" and being assured that there

is to be an inestimable compensation for all earthly tribulations, is satisfied to endure until his God gives him eternal deliverance.

III. THE UPRIGHT MAN IS SHOWN THE SALVATION OF THE LORD, WHICH IS REALLY THE SECRET OF HIS SATISFACTION.

1. God shows him personal salvation from sin. Much is said about the difficulties of living a Christian life. Some seem to succeed but for a short time. God, however, often shows His children how it may be done for the period of a long lifetime.

2. God shows him the truth of His word. The veteran of the cross has had time to fully test the promises of the Scriptures, to see the working of divine power, and to realize the blessedness of a godly life.

3. God shows him the power of the Gospel to save mankind. The aged saint has seen several generations appear and develop into manhood and womanhood. He has had ample time and opportunity to observe the course in life of both the pious and the godless. He has learned from observation the inevitable results both of virtue and of sin. He has witnessed the transformation of character wrought by the Gospel of Christ. He has marked the civilizing influence of Christianity upon the nations of the earth. He is satisfied that the religion of Christ "is the power of God unto salvation to every one that believeth," and he is ready to say with the venerable Simeon: "Lord, now lettest thou thy servant depart in peace," etc. Luke 2:29-32.

The Saint's Repose

"He giveth his beloved sleep." — Ps. 127:2

Let us notice.

I. GOD'S BELOVED.—"HE GIVETH HIS BELOVED SLEEP."

1. It is a doctrine universally accepted and believed that God loves all men—Bible doctrine. "For God so loved the world."

2. But the words of our text, as well as numerous other passages of Scripture, teach that there are those for whom God entertains a special affection, and peculiar attachment. They are His by special, and most tender ties.

(*a*) *His by purchase.* "Not with corruptible things." (b) *His by regeneration.* "Of water and of the Spirit." (c) *His by adoption.* "Have the Spirit of adoption."—are His children—as such he loves them. (d) *His in love.* They reciprocate His love to them. (e) *His in obedience.* It is their meat and drink. (f) *They trust in Him.* They make the Lord their portion, and His glory their constant aim. (g) *They trust in Him.* They make the Lord their portion, and His glory their constant aim. (g) *They live not for this world, nor for self, but for God and for those things which are above.* Satan and the wicked world hate and persecute them. But they are God's "Beloved" still. Are we His Beloved?

II. HIS GIFT TO THEM. "He giveth His beloved *sleep.*" Sleep, repose, satisfaction—He does so.

1. *With reference to Temporal things.*

2. *With reference to Spiritual things.*

3. *With reference to Eternal things.* He gives them sleep —satisfaction.

1. *In the knowledge of His redeeming love.*

2. *In the consciousness of pardoned sin, acceptance and adoption.*

3. *In the supply of all their needs.*

4. *In His exceeding great and precious promises.*

5. *In frequent foretastes of joy to come.* They "shall be satisfied." Their cup of joy often "runneth over." And this he gives them—a gift unmerited, freely. The world and the Devil gives disquiet, a certain fearful looking for the judgment, pain, and sorrow, and anguish and an aching, condemning conscience; an eternal waking in torment and misery. But God "giveth His Beloved sleep," rest. In this

life, and after their day of earthly toil is over, then will come the sleep of death—only a sleep. Our Lord, himself calls it so. In speaking of the death of Jairus' daughter, "The damsel is not dead but asleep in Jesus, blessed sleep." Death, a sleep? Then, indeed, is there in the death of God's beloved nothing terrible, its sting is gone, and it comes but as a friend to close their eyes and relieve them of the toils and ills, and sorrows of this sinful, troublesome world.

III. HE GIVETH HIS BELOVED SLEEP.

These words come to us today, in the midst of our sorrow and tears, teaching us important lessons, both of admonition and comfort. They remind us of the very significant fact,

1. *That there is a dark night coming.* The night of death.

2. *Of the importance of preparation.*

3. *That there will be an awaking.* We shall not sleep forever. Shall we awake with Dives, the rich man, in eternal torment, or shall it be with Lazarus in Abraham's bosom?

4. *That there will be a happy meeting in the morning.* When Christ shall gather his own from the east and the west, and from the north and the south, and they shall sit down with Him in the Kingdom. God's Beloved will all meet again?

Jesus Calling Children through the Angel of Death

"Suffer the little children to come unto me. . . ." — Mark 10:14

"Little traveler Zionward,
    Thou hast entered into rest,
In the kingdom of your Lord.
    In the mansions of the blest;
There, to welcome, Jesus waits,
    There a crown of glory win;
Lift your heads, ye golden gates!
    Let the little traveler in."

Having made a few changes, these words of the poet apply

to the present case. The dear child, sleeping so peacefully in this casket amid garlands of flowers, has entered into rest in the mansions of the blest. Jesus has welcomed this little traveler after a very brief pilgrimage on earth to his heavenly home. He has said to these bereaved parents, "Suffer this child to come unto me and forbid him not;" etc.

I. JESUS HAS CALLED OUR DEPARTED CHILDREN.

1. *Behold His love to children.* They are His favorites. We sometimes speak of this or that person as a great friend of the children. Jesus, however, is absolutely the children's greatest friend. He loves them dearly. When on earth he called them to Him, laid His hands on them, folded them lovingly in His arms and gave them His benediction. Matt. 18:10.

2. *Behold His claim on all our children.* (a) *They are an heritage of the Lord.*—Ps. 127:3. God Himself must give them, or a man will die childless. The great Napoleon, with all his sinful care in regard to this matter, died without an heir, and could not create a dynasty. Job acknowledged this fact, saying of his lost children, "The Lord gave." (b) *He has redeemed them.* Jesus suffered and died to save them from the curse of the law and eternal death. If they die before they have arrived at years of accountability, they are not guilty of personal sin. In this their so-called state of innocence they are incapable of moral obligation. They inherit, it is true, the fallen nature of the human race; but they also enjoy the gracious benefits of the atonement made by Jesus, although they are incapable of employing the appointed means of grace. (c) *They have been given to the Lord.* Christian parents consecrate their children to God by means of Holy Baptism.

3. *Behold His promise to children.* "Of such is the kingdom of God." "O mother," exclaimed a little girl, running into her mother's sick-room on her return from church, "I have heard the child's gospel today!" She had heard this passage in Mark's gospel.

II. THE CONSOLATION FOR BEREAVED PARENTS.

1. *These words shed light on the death of children.* They have gone to Jesus. He has taken the dear lambs to His bosom. H. W. Beecher once said: "I have been called to give dear ones. Not once nor twice, nor thrice, but many times. I have sent my children on before me. Once, wading knee-deep in the snow, I buried my earliest. It was March, and dreary and shivering and awful; and then the doctrine that Christ sat in an eternal summer of love, and that my child was not buried, but had gone up to One that loved it better than I, was the only comfort I had."

2. *These words call for humble submission.* "Forbid them not." Should bereaved parents not heed this word of the blessed Master? Such parents should be willing and ready to give up their child to Jesus, who has more right to its presence and affection than they. They should feel that the hour cannot be untimely, which numbers it with all the radiant spirits around the throne of God. They should feel that the great dresser of God's vineyard knows best when to transplant his tender shoots.

3. *These words give to bereaved parents a blessed hope.* We cannot believe "that death ends all." We will go to our departed children. They have but crossed the river of death a few days before us. We shall soon embark, and if we have been faithful and obedient, we shall meet and greet them in the beautiful and happy home above.

The Great Meeting

"Prepare to meet thy God." — Amos 4:12

Because of their incorrigible sins the Israelites are commanded to meet their God.

I. WE MUST ALL ONE DAY MEET OUR GOD IN JUDGMENT.

Firstly: *Scripture declares it.* "He hath appointed a day."

Acts 17:31. "The day cometh that shall burn as an oven." Mal. 4:1. See also II Peter 3:7; Matt. 25:32; Rom. 2:5; Lev. 6:17; Rev. 20:12. Secondly: *The punishment of vice and the reward of virtue demand it.* Consider the present, apparently chaotic state of the moral world, crimes now go unpunished. Thirdly: *The holy character of God demands it.* He will destroy sin from his universe. Deut. 24:16; Prov. 6:16; 19; I Kings 14:22. Fourthly: *Our present state of probation anticipates it.*

II. A PREPARATION IS NECESSARY TO MEET OUR GOD WITH JOY. Firstly: *Many of us are not in a fit state to meet Him,* because of sinful indulgence, living as though there were no God to meet. Secondly: *Even those who profess to be followers of Christ need to prepare.* Our lamps should be always *burning.* Thirdly: *We cannot tell how soon the meeting may take place.* Fourthly: *The consequences of being unprepared, when we meet our God, will be awful.* "Depart," etc.

III. THERE IS A WAY TO PREPARE FOR THAT GREAT MEETING. This is implied. "Believe on the Lord Jesus Christ," etc. First: *There must be repentance for sin.* Job. 33:27; Prov. 28:13; Ps. 38:18; Jer. 3:21; Rom. 12:9. Secondly: *There must be a forsaking of sin.* Ps. 34:14; II Tim. 2:19. Thirdly: *We must come unto God,* sinful *as we are, for forgiveness,* depending *entirely on the sacrifice of Christ.* "He died the just for the unjust," etc. Eph. 2:13-18; Heb. 9:15, 12:24. Fourthly: *We must then walk in newness of life*—growing in sanctification. Remember, we must meet God in judgment. We cannot tell how soon the meeting may take place. Therefore prepare.

Human Life in the Light of Christ's Appearing

"Lord, now lettest thou thy servant depart in peace, according
to thy word: for my eyes have seen thy salvation."
— Luke 2:29, 30

The words of the venerable Simeon when he saw the
Christ. There are moments in life when, if we do not adopt
his language, we feel as he felt. The question is, have we
his aim and hope before us? Some avoid that question, and
no wonder. The light, so beautiful and pleasant to the
eye, is painful to the disordered brain. The evil doer shuns
the light. The man who has no love to Christ shuns the
thought of him.

Our subject is *human life in the light of Christ's appearing;*
the light in which Simeon saw it. These words were uttered
when Simeon saw the Christ. That sight only could satisfy
him and give him rest. The parents were presenting the child.
Simeon "a just and devout man," etc.—no matter, therefore,
what else he was—greets him. He comes before us here as
a man who has *discovered the great problem of life, and has
solved it: he offers devout praise* for the solution he has
found: he can now *depart in peace and joy.* There is in him,
therefore, all that there needs be in us to make life bright
and cheerful: its experiences plain, its close a peaceful departure.

I. WHAT THE GREAT PURPOSE OF LIFE. Simeon
waited for the Savior. His pious soul looked to him as to his
highest good. Apart from him life was empty, purposeless
and vain. The purpose of his being could be reached only
by knowing the Savior. He waited for his appearing, therefore, with holy lingering, especially as it was revealed to him
that he should see Christ before he died. One would not
judge that this was the purpose of life to look at many about
us, who think and act as the children of the moment, with
no lofty well-defined object before them. This life the vesti-
bule to the eternal life: we are here to secure that eternal
life, though so many live for the perishing. This life not
in us: sin has corrupted us: it is the gift of God. Christ the

fountain of purity and health. To win Christ, therefore, the purpose of life. Our joy in time and eternity depends on our knowing Him and becoming like Him. Life has been wasted and worse, if Christ is not ours.

II. The purpose of life being reached, THE EXPERI-ENCES OF LIFE AWAKEN GRATITUDE. Simeon's hope fulfilled. Our text; heartier words of praise than ever before escaped his lips. He held in his arms and pressed to his heart the Savior. The mysteries of the past were rolled away. This the feeling of the new-born Christian in looking back on the past. The past dark to some; awakens doubt and rebellion in others; in the Christian heart it awakens gratitude. There is a point in ascending a mountain when you see the skill of the engineer in the strangely constructed path. Simeon was at that point; a halo of light was about the past; what flood of light the cross throws on life! Though Simeon's hopes and prayers were answered, yet the answer was very unlike what he expected. God's answers to our prayers are widely different from what we expect. A fresh tie yonder is often his call to heavenly-mindedness—disappointment, his call to us to trust in Him.

III. THE CLOSE OF SUCH A LIFE, A DEPARTURE. Simeon saw his hope in that child, and all the fetters that bound him to the earth were snapped. We have a clearer light than Simeon had. Death peaceful to many to whom it is not a departure. To the Christian it is a loosing the cable and gliding peacefully into the haven of rest—a going home.

The New Jerusalem

"Behold I make all things new." — Rev. 21:5

It might be interesting to consider the changes this terrestial globe must undergo, as a part of the *all things* to be made new. But our purpose is not to be interesting but comforting, not to conjecture but to assure. Therefore we wish to view the matter of transformation as it especially effects God's children.

I. THE FIRST EVIDENCE I GET IN SUPPORT OF THE TEXT COMES IN THESE WORDS:—*"There shall be no more curse."* This is a clear assertion that *sin* in any of its forms, shapes, disguises, shall not exist in the New Jerusalem. The curse of sin hangs over this earth, man has fallen under it, his nobility has been striken down, his glory wrested from him, his diadem destroyed. Man always feels the striving for mastery in himself.—"O wretched man that I am," etc.—Rom. 7:24. But all things are to be made new. The rolling drums of warfare, temporal and spiritual, will cease to beat. The oath, the foul remark, withered beauty, fallen virtue, etc., will not be thrown there.—"There shall be no more *curse*."

II. THERE SHALL BE NEITHER SORROW, CRY-ING, NOR PAIN. The causes now for sorrow are multiform. They are like ambushed archers with the arrow upon the string, ready at any moment to pierce the sensibilities of our nature. Here we are summoned into the furnaces of trial, some of which are mingled afflictions of body and soul. Here the tear will start; Rachael will weep for her children and David will mourn for Absalom, etc. There the golden pave-ment will not be stained with a single tear-drop.—"God shall wipe away all tears."

III. "THERE SHALL BE NO NIGHT THERE." Night has its symbolism,—darkness, ignorance, error, even mystery are symboled by the night. Night never comes but it taunts man with his imperfection—he cannot continuously endure. In that city we shall not need the night either for rest or instruction. All thing will be explained. John 13:7.

IV. "THE CITY HATH NO NEED OF THE SUN." A change indeed great. The earthly sun—the necessary fount of light and life. Ten thousand mouths laugh upon tree and springing grass, when he pours his vital warmth upon the earth. Then its presence will be superflous. "The Lamb shall be the light thereof." "In his light shall we see light." We can not fully realize it now. We know not what a volume of ineffable light our God can weave out of Bethlehem, Gethsemane, Calvary, Bethany; they will all be blended into that new light of which the Lamb in the midst of the throne is the source and fountain.

V. "THERE SHALL BE NO MORE DEATH." No river of *death* here. It is the state and condition of perpetual life. The inhabitants are not there "in bondage through fear of death." A Christian lady was upon her death-bed; her brother taking leave of her, to return to his distant home, said: "Farewell sister, we shall, probably, never meet again in the land of the living!" "Brother," said she, "I trust we *shall* meet in the land of the living, we are now in the land of the dying." How true! Earth is honeycombed with graves. Death's harvest is always ripe and ripening. His day of operation is however too close. To the Christian all these transformations are more blessed; death is only the passage from the old to the new. The gain is immense. It is poverty, suddenly banished by coming into possession of untold wealth; it is sorrow effectually arrested by the greeting of the soul by indescribable joy. It is the night shades scattered by the refulgent beams of glory's eternal day.

Shall We Know Each Other in Heaven?

"For what is our hope, or joy, or crown of rejoicing?..."
— I Thess. 2:19

From the records we have, we would judge the church at Thessalonica to be almost a model one. Paul, who was the active agent in its planting, seems to have entertained a very warm affection for the Christians there, and often longed to see them again in the flesh. Circumstances took place through which all hopes of visiting the church again seem to be blasted, and in writing this Epistle, he speaks of his disappointment in this matter, but asserts his deriving comfort from the thought that if they should never meet one another again in this world, they would meet one another in the better land. Such a hope animated him, and has animated all Christians in all ages when parting with Christian friends. Have we sure grounds on which to base such a hope? We think we have. Admitting the doctrine of the resurrection of the body to be a settled fact, and that all Christians shall meet together in the heavenly mansions, the question becomes one of deep interest: Shall we know one another then? Our affirmative answer is based upon the following grounds:

I. Apart from direct scriputral teachings, it has ever been, and is now, the general sentiment of mankind. Men of all creeds and shades of belief, have agreed on this point. Homer, Socrates and Philo—men of heathern antiquity believed in and wrote about it. The general agreement of all men, while not a direct argument is yet not an argument to be cast aside, for where is there a doctrine on which such an agreement exists but what is true?

II. The doctrine of future recognition has ever been a precious doctrine to which Christians of all ages have tenaciously held to and taught. The Jews have always believed in it. How common the expression among them: "gathered unto the fathers." Abraham wanted his family all buried together here, as they would live together in the future world. The New Testament Christians never doubted the doctrine. The early reformers boldly preached it. All along the ages down to the present time, this belief is common to Christians of every age, country, religion or denomination.

III. The nature of the resurrection body warrants us in giving an affirmative answer to the question. True, the body will be somewhat different, from what it is now. It will be immortal, spiritual, glorious, yet it will be the same body. Admit the resurrection of the same body—We admit future recognition, for the changes wrought in the body will not, in the least, destroy identity. But our greatest proof resides in

IV. The Scriptural statement which, to our minds, are conclusive in proving the doctrine. (1) II Sam. 12:22. David clearly shows by his language that the prospect of a future *reunion* with his child was a source of great comfort to him. (2) Matt. 8:11. These words carry the idea of there being a *banquet* in heaven. This certainly implies recognition and enjoyment of each other's society. If we don't know the guests would it be heaven to us? (3) Matt. 17:1-6. Moses and Elias were at once recognized by the disciples though they had never seen them before. (4) Luke 16:22. This passage clearly teaches future recognition. The rich man had fulfilled in his experience that awful prediction of Christ. See Luke 13:28, 29. (5) Religion, instead of destroying social affections, purifies and strengthens them. God has planted in our very natures these affections of our loved ones, and this *yearning* in our hearts for future reunion and recognition is of God. We are to be social beings in heaven. Will God gratify or destroy this *yearning* for future joy in heaven in union with those of earth we love? The language of every bereaved Christian heart, when death took a Christian friend away, has been "I shall go to him." (6) Religion, by its very nature, binds all of God's people in one strongbond of union. Shall that bond of love and fellowship be broken by death? If so, then death, instead of being a blessing to the Christian, becomes a curse. (7) Paul says: "Now I know in part, but then shall I know even as I am known." Now, the simple question is—Shall we know *less* in heaven?

Conclusion—The doctrine being true, it should lead us: (1) To earnestly seek the salvation of all whom we love. (2) To live in concord, peace and unity with all lovers of Jesus. (3) To be more and more heavenly-minded. (4) To be comforted in all bereavements. When Christians die it is simply their going home to rest. When we die, if we are faithful, we shall meet them and recognize them, and share the joys of heaven forever with them.

Watching for the Master

"Blessed are those servants, whom the Lord when he cometh shall find watching." — Luke 12:37

In the context Christ charges his disciples not to set their affections on the things of this world, etc. He here charges them to get ready, and to keep in readiness for His coming, when all those who have laid up their treasure in Heaven shall enter on the full enjoyment of it.

I. THE LORD AND HIS SERVANTS.

1. *Christ himself is the Lord and Master.*

2. *We all are His servants, either faithful or unfaithful, diligent or slothful.* All are alike, called to serve. All are under obligation to Him, and alike responsible to Him for their conduct.

II. THE LORD AS ABSENT FROM HIS SERVANTS.

He has gone up on high. Is absent in person—present in Spirit. Christ our Master, though now thus absent, will return again. He will come to take cognizance of His servants, to inspect their work and give him their reward. This may be applied to His coming.

1. *In death, and,* 2. *In judgment.*—The day of His coming will be a critical one, a day of the closest scrutiny. When the secrets of all hearts shall be disclosed, and every man shall be judged and rewarded according to that which he hath done.

III. THE TIME OF HIS COMING AS UNCERTAIN.

It will be in the night, which indicates that many will be found sleeping. It may be in the second watch, or in the third watch.

1. *His coming to us at death is certain,* but not the time when, where, and in what manner.

2. *This be-speaks not only the uncertainty of the time of His coming,* but also the prevailing security of the greatest part of men, who are unthinking, so that, whenever he comes

it will be "at an hour when" etc. and will be to them a great and terrible surprise. "Death enters and there's no defense."

IV. THAT THE LORD EXPECTS AND REQUIRES, THAT, WHENEVER HE COMES, HIS SERVANTS MAY BE READY TO RECEIVE HIM, OR, RATHER, TO BE RECEIVED BY HIM.

That they be found with their loins girt about, and at work. That they be found watching and waiting, with their lamps trimmed and burning. This preparation or readiness for the coming of the Lord consists,

1. *In repentance.* "Repent for the Kingdom," etc.

2. *In a change of the heart.* Regeneration—"Except a man," etc.

3. *In a holy and devoted life.* "Blessed are the pure."

The true Christian or servant of Christ, though he knows not the time of His coming, is always ready. "I am now ready to be offered," etc.

V. THE BLESSEDNESS OF THOSE SERVANTS WHO ARE FOUND WATCHING.

1. *They are blessed and happy already here in his service and in watching for Him.*

2. *They are blessed and happy at the time of His coming, when the words of His approval shall greet them.* "Well done thou good," etc.

3. *They are blessed because they enter into rest.* "There remaineth a rest," etc.

4. *They are blessed because they shall be with Christ.* "Where I am there shall also my servant be."

5. *They are blessed because they shall inherit the Kingdom.* "Come ye blessed."

6. *They are blessed because they shall have an everlasting feast of joy.* "Sit down to meat."

7. *They are blessed because the highest honors shall be conferred upon them.* Their Lord shall "serve them." Have we the assurance of this?

A Whole Family in Heaven

"And the Lord said unto Noah, Come thou and all thy house into the ark." — Gen. 7:1

The family a divine organism: therefore, to be perpetuated forever. Many suggestions in the Scriptures combine with the deep instincts of nature to teach that we shall know our kindred in heaven and be associated with them in special affection as here.

I. God in the Scriptures deals with families both in saving and destroying.

II. Noah's obedience of faith the salvation of his household. Special obligations on heads of families to bring the household to Christ.

III. Unspeakable joy of the family reunion after the storms and separations of earth. What greetings! what memories! what unalloyed fellowship and blissful employments!

Application.—There are whole families here in Christ, and there in heaven. Some are divided. Shall any be left out?

Man's March to the Grave

"For I know that thou wilt bring me to death, and to the house appointed for all the living." — Job 30:23

This is the language of Job—the language of a severely afflicted man. At this time every visible thing which surrounded him bore the flaming inscription of "Ichabod"—the glory is departed. His earthly possessions had departed; his children had departed; his servants, of whom he had a large number, had departed; his wife had departed, for she turned against him, saying: "Dost thou still retain thine integrity? Curse God and die." Even his most intimate friends had departed, for they charged him with hypocrisy and deceit. It must have seemed to him the beginning of the end.

The text is applicable to every human being. We are all subject to death; we are all mortal. God's decree has gone forth, sealing man's doom in respect to his mortality. Gen. 3:19; Rom. 5:12; Heb. 9:27.

EVERY MAN IS MARCHING TO THE GRAVE. However robust the constitution, and strong the frame, and long the conflict—at last the preacher has preached his last sermon, the teacher has taught his last lesson, the statesman has played his last diplomatic role, the general must resign his command, and the man of business has made his last bargain. And it is well that immortality is not for the imperfect life in these earthly surroundings. "The average life," says Pastor Glover, "is long enough for the average power of enjoying it." It is well that this life should be "rounded off by sleep."

1. THE GRAVE IS THE APPOINTED HOUSE OF ALL LIVING. It is not a matter of chance that we go to the grave. The Great Arbiter of life has so ordained it. How solemn the thought, that such a home is the goal of every man! "For all that sit on thrones; for all that move in the halls of music and pleasure; for all that roll along in splendid carriages; for all in the marts of business, in the low scenes of dissipation, and in the sanctuary of God; for every one who is young, and every one who is aged, this is the home!" (Dr. A. Barnes.) It is God's hand that leads us to the grave and puts us in that narrow bed.

2. THIS DESTINATION OF MAN IS ALMOST ENTIRELY IGNORED. We live and move in these earthly scenes, as though we were to live and abide here forever. Some unusual circumstance in the death of some fellow-man may arrest our attention; the sad occasion may, perhaps, draw our thoughts from their ordinary occupations, and awaken frightful images of the grave and eternity. But these thoughts soon vanish in life's turmoil. The irrevocable sentence is forgotten only too soon. "It is appointed unto men once to die."

3. THIS DESTINATION OUGHT TO MAKE EVERY MAN FEEL THAT LIFE IS A SERIOUS THING. Let us therefore be careful that we do not commit the error of the mass of our fellow-beings, who treat time as if it were eternity, and eternity as if it were time. The thought of death should

wake those wasteful of the precious hours and days of life. It says, "Awake thou that sleepest, and arise from the dead." It bids us live while we live, and work while it is called day.

4. THIS DESTINATION OUGHT TO COMFORT THE AFFLICTED. Faint not, be not disheartened, sorrowing and afflicted brother and sister! "The light affliction is but for a moment." Trials are only mortal. Death is to the suffering and bereaved Christian eternal gain. To him death seems the

"Kind umpire of men's miseries,
  Which, with sweet enlargement, does dismiss us hence."

5. THIS DESTINATION OUGHT TO IMPEL US TO LAY HOLD OF ETERNAL LIFE. The thought of our impending death should awaken a desire for a blissful immortality. It should spur us on in every holy endeavor to gain the haven of eternal peace and rest.

The Close of Summer

"The summer is ended." — Jer. 8:20

I. A fact in nature.

Procession of the seasons never comes to a halt. Moving panorama of nature's miracles shifts its scenes. Summer's work, its fruit, past.

(a) The summer has its own beauty, joy and use—never fails. Always essentially the same. Yet the same summer never returns.

(b) A time of glowing sun and growing crops. The spring time and the autumn cannot do summer's work.

II. In human life. Its summer has closed with some special opportunities, brightest, most genial influences for religious growth and usefulness. Autumn at hand. Should show ripened fruits. If you have sown in tears during the summer, you may be sure of reaping with joy in the autumn. Is harvest ready or only withering leaves? The days grow briefer.

We Are Not Left Comfortless

"I will not leave you comfortless." — John 14:18

Know ye not that a great man in Israel has fallen? Many hearts are sad. The words of the text were uttered by Jesus in the presence of Calvary and Gethsemane. What tenderness! How does Jesus comfort in all ages? How can He comfort these mourning hearts today?

1. By His own tender sympathy and help. Touched with a feeling of our own infirmity. A friend. His suffering for us. His grace.

2. By giving His spirit, the Comforter.

3. By gracious assurance concerning those who die in the Lord. "Blessed are they who die in the Lord." "To die is gain." "The eye hath not seen," etc. "And we shall be satisfied," etc.

4. By making our affliction a wholesome discipline. "Light afflictions." All things work for good, etc.

5. By the hope of reunion.

Friends, you who are so afflicted today, are not strangers to His grace. He will not leave you desolate. All the sources of comfort are open to you. O ye children, remember your father's God is a special friend to the young. You have been left a rich legacy in the memories that cluster, etc.

Friends, members of this sorely afflicted congregation, let not this occasion pass away unimproved. May this affliction work out for you, etc. How his life, his death, should inspire us to rededicate ourselves to the work of Christ on earth.

May God help us to be, as our brother was, faithful unto death.

Death Always in Our Path

"There is but a step between me and death." — I Sam. 20:3

We associate death only with conscious danger, with sickness, decay, old age, etc.; and hence, while young, vigorous, unexposed, if we think of death at all, it is as a *far-off* enemy, an event that lies in the dim, distant *future*. Fatal mistake!

I. Death is as nigh to us in youth as in extreme old age.

II. Death is as nigh to us in the full flush of health as in the hour of wasted strength and consuming sickness.

III. Death is as nigh to us in the moment of seeming security as in the hour of extremest seen peril.

IV. Death is as nigh to us in the mart of business, in the scene of thoughtless revelry, in the haunt of dissipation, in the experience of a thoughtless, prayerless, ungodly life, as in the quiet home, the sanctuary, the hour of solemn reflection, the sick-chamber, the dying bed!

V. Death is as nigh to us in the seclusion of our chamber, in the hour of sleep, in the circle of loving friends, as when we tread the rough ways of active life and face the conflicts and the perils of society.

Yet how few believe that death is *always* near them—in their very path, by they very sides, in every step of life! Whitfield, in one of his sermons, uses this illustration to show the sinner's imminent danger.

"See yonder *blind* man, with feeble step approaching a fearful precipice. He pauses on its very brink, as if he felt an instinct of danger. But only for a moment. He lifts his cane and his right foot, and they are suspended over the giddy precipice!" At this instance Garrick, the actor, who happened to be present, was so carried away with the vivid description that he rose and shouted, "By heaven, he's gone!"

Substitute death for that precipice, and you have the fact of the case in regard to every one of us. Our path across the plain of probation lies along the very brink of that precipice —and any day, any hour, in any experience, at home or abroad, in youth or middle life, or old age, thoughtless or prayerful, ready or not ready, our plans of life accomplished or incomplete—in a moment, the fatal step may be taken and we drop into eternity!

Posthumous Eloquence

"He being dead, yet speaketh." — Heb. 11:4

The eloquence of life and the eloquence after life are nearly one, the latter for the most part a prolonged reverberation. The life may be still a living epistle, not dependent upon monumental marble, nor the book memoirs. There are, however, special values attaching to the echoes of the life after it has closed on earth.

I. Speaking through the charitable memoirs of men, kindred, friends, the church, the community—by word, work, example.

II. Speaketh in testimony and vindication of the truths, the cause for which the life stood as an exponent. A completed argument, the peroration, the most forcible part and the most lasting in impression.

III. Pre-eminently Christian faith gives posthumous power to the life. "By *it* he [Abel], being dead, yet speaketh." Agnosticism, infidelity, pessimism, worldliness, selfishness, in any form not only winds up in despair, but leaves no echo that men care to listen to. Christian faith, as the soul of the Christian's life, is immortal and perennial in influence and fruitfulness. It reappears in children and children's children. It adds continually to the witnesses summoned by the Church in her vindication, adds undying elements to the Church's endless pilgrim song.

The Certainty of Death

"It is appointed unto men once to die, but after this the judgment." — Heb. 9:27

I. DEATH.

1. *The certainty and universality of the fact.*

2. *The uncertainty of the time.*

3. *Knowledge of the fact, not its realization.* We know these things about death, but do not heed them as we should.

We live as though we were to be here always. Let us lay these solemn facts to heart.

4. *Death as privation.* A time of solemn farewell, when earthly riches take to themselves wings and flee away, earthly aims are shattered, earthly friendships are severed.

5. *Death as a journey.* A time of yet more solemn expectations. "We go hence"—where? To judgment.

II. JUDGMENT.

1. *On whom?* All persons, small and great.

2. *On what?* All acts, words, desires, motives.

3. *By whom?* By Jesus Christ, now offered to us as our Savior and Advocate.

4. *By what rule?* By the law revealed in his Word, which is within reach of all.

5. *With what result?* Eternal blessedness, or eternal woe to every soul of man.

III. HOPE IN DEATH.

1. *Its source.* Not our own goodness. But God's mercy in Christ.

2. *Its evidence.* Not our willingness to die. This often means no more than that we desire cessation of our bodily pains. But our trust in Christ, as evidenced by our active and passive submission to his will.

IV. THE MOURNER'S COMFORT IN CHRISTIAN-ITY. There is no other source of comfort of which we know than the gospel of Christ, which reveals—

1. Death as the gate of life to Christ's people.

2. The ministry of sorrow for our purifying.

An Unexpected Requisition

"Thou fool! this night thy soul shall be required of thee."
— Luke 12:20

Three questions:
1. What is the *soul?*
II. What is meant by its being *required?*
III. Why was this man a *fool?*

I. *Soul*=Life. It is the REAL LIFE, because.

1. It is the seat of all life's *motives.* "The soul uses intellect and will as hands and feet" (Emerson). The soul really does all that we consciously do.

2. It is the seat of all *feelings.* There is no physical sensation ever, except as the soul is alert in the body.

3. It is the seat of all *responsibility.*

4. It is the only *enduring* part—immortal.

II. The soul REQUIRED.

1. Its *motives exposed.* No more concealment from others, from ourselves.

2. Its *feeling unchecked.* No more moral anesthesia; no secular diversion from the sting of conscience, the bitterness of sinful memory. The soul like an exposed nerve.

3. Its *accounts audited.* Engrossed in eternal records.

4. Its *immortal character and destiny fixed.*

III. The man was a FOOL, because

1. He did not realize (a) That his soul was his real life, but thought it consisted in the "abundance of the things" that he possessed.

2. He did not realize (b) That his soul might at any moment be required of him.

The Progressive March of Death's Conqueror

"He shall swallow up death in victory." — Isa. 25:8

In nature God is constantly "swallowing up death in victory." In spring He opens a million graves, and floods the world with life. Indeed everywhere He makes death the minister of life. Death generates, nurtures and develops life. But the text points us to his *victory* over the mortality of man, and let us trace the march of the triumphant conqueror in this direction.

I. WE SEE HIS FIRST CONQUEST IN THE RESURRECTION OF CHRIST. The strongest victim death ever had was Christ. In slaying Him, he slayed the world, he slayed humanity. The Jewish Sanhedrin cooperated with the Roman power and did all they could to keep the victim in the grave. But the Conqueror of death appeared, invaded the territory of mortality, broke open the prison doors, snapped the fetters, and led the prisoner into a new and triumphant life.

II. WE SEE HIS NEXT CONQUEST IN DESTROYING IN HUMANITY THE FEAR OF DEATH. The essence, the sting, the venom, the power of death, are not in the mere article of dissolution of soul and body, but in the thoughts and feelings of men regarding the event. To overcome, therefore, in the human mind all terrible thoughts and apprehensive feelings concerning death, is the most effective way to triumph over it. This is to bruise the very head of the serpent. This the Great Conqueror has done in millions of instances, is doing now, and will do till the end of time. "Forasmuch then as children are partakers of flesh and blood, he also Himself likewise took part in the same, that through death he might destroy him that hath the power of death, that is, the devil." Every true Christian shouts victory even in the very article of dissolution. "O death, where is thy sting?" "O grave, where is thy victory."

III. WE SEE HIS CROWNING CONQUEST IN THE GENERAL RESURRECTION. First: There is nothing increditable in the general resurrection of the dead. Secondly: There are circumstances that render the event exceedingly probable. Thirdly: The declarations of God render it absolutely certain. "Behold, I show thee a mystery; we shall not all sleep, we shall be changed," etc.

Death Not Destruction, but a Step in the Process of Development

"I am not come to destroy, but to fulfill." — Matt. 5:17

As Christ said this of Himself, so we can say of death, "I am not come to destroy," for we observe that

I. LIFE IN ITS PRIMAL FORM DOES NOT CONTINUE TO EXIST IN THAT FORM, but is a development (as seen in the individual).

1. In mental growth—"When I was a child."

2. In soul culture—till we "have a desire to depart."

3. That points upward, *beyond* the present, for have we not indescribable longings to know, to do, what seems so infinitely beyond present capabilities?

II. LIFE, THEREFORE, IS NOT SUFFICIENT IN

1. Opportunities. 2. Duties. 3. Possibilities, for we are

III. LONGING TO FULFILL—

To become conscious of completeness, and, therefore, is

IV. DEATH THE RELEASE to

1. Life's "reserve of goodness;" to

2. Its completeness (which are formed in)

3. Christ.

Appropriate Texts for Funeral Services

Job 1:21	Matthew 25:23
Ephesians 5:10	I John 3:2
Hebrew 11:16	Romans 2:7
I Thess. 4:13-18	Luke 18:16
Revelation 14:1	Psalm 39:9
Job 16:22	Isaiah 55:8
Hebrew 11:13-16	I Chronicles 29:15
Matthew 14:12	Psalm 127:15
I Peter 4:7	Genesis 43:14
Jeremiah 15:9	Matthew 9:24
Psalm 90:12	Exodus 22:29
Job 30:23	Lamentations 5:15
Genesis 47:9	Isaiah 51:12
Micah 2:10	Hosea 6:1
Acts 7:55-60	Job 10:20
Psalm 21:5	John 14:4
John 4:50	Revelation 12:5
Ecclesiastes 7:1	Psalm 16:6
Psalm 48:14	Psalm 103:13
Ecclesiastes 9:10	Acts 2:39
Daniel 12:3	John 20:13
II Timothy 1:12	Matthew 18:3
I Samuel 3:18	Hebrew 13:14
Lamentations 1:9	I Kings 2:2
Hebrew 4:9	Psalm 39:3
Revelation 3:5	II Timothy 4:6
Malachi 3:2	Isaiah 57:2
Revelation 22:4	John 9:4
II Corinthians 5:8-10	Revelation 21:4
Revelation 2:40	Psalm 90:3
Amos 4:12	Jeremiah 9:21
Psalm 84:48	Psalm 89:48
I Peter 1:3, 4	Zechariah 1:5
Galatians 6:7, 8	Ecclesiastes 1:4
II Chronicles 34:3	Ecclesiastes 12:7
Luke 12:40	Genesis 27:2

I Corinthians 7:31
Daniel 12:13
Ecclesiastes 9:5
Isaiah 38:11
Job 5:26
Proverbs 10:27
Proverbs 16:32
Daniel 12:2
Psalm 102:24
Ecclesiastes 9:12
Psalm 90:10
II Corinthians 5:1
II Timothy 4:7, 8
Lamentations 4:18
John 11:25

Psalm 35:14
II Samuel 19:34
Psalm 49:17
John 6:39
I Peter 1:9
John 12:26
I Samuel 15:32
Psalm 90:9
Job 7:1
Job 14:10
Ecclesiastes 7:2
II Timothy 1:10
II Kings 20:1
Ecclesiastes 3:20
Revelation 14:13